The Human Rights Issue

ISSUES

Volume 120

Series Editor

Craig Donnellan

Assistant Editor

Lisa Firth

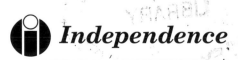
Independence
Educational Publishers

First published by Independence
PO Box 295
Cambridge CB1 3XP
England

British Library Cataloguing in Publication Data
The Human Rights Issue – (Issues Series)
I. Donnellan, Craig II. Series
323

ISBN 1 86168 353 7

Printed in Great Britain
MWL Print Group Ltd

Layout by
Lisa Firth

Cover
The illustration on the front cover is by
Simon Kneebone.

CONTENTS

Chapter One: Young People's Rights

Chapter Two: Human and Civil Rights

Introduction

The Human Rights Issue is the one hundred and twentieth volume in the **Issues** series. The aim of this series is to offer up-to-date information about important issues in our world.

The Human Rights Issue looks at the rights of young people, and at the relationship between human and civil rights.

The information comes from a wide variety of sources and includes:
Government reports and statistics
Newspaper reports and features
Magazine articles and surveys
Website material
Literature from lobby groups
and charitable organisations.

It is hoped that, as you read about the many aspects of the issues explored in this book, you will critically evaluate the information presented. It is important that you decide whether you are being presented with facts or opinions. Does the writer give a biased or an unbiased report? If an opinion is being expressed, do you agree with the writer?

The Human Rights Issue offers a useful starting-point for those who need convenient access to information about the many issues involved. However, it is only a starting-point. Following each article is a URL to the relevant organisation's website, which you may wish to visit for further information.

*****

Frequently asked questions about children's rights

The Children's Rights Alliance for England is often asked questions about children's human rights. We have provided brief answers to 11 of those most frequently asked

What are children's rights?

Children's rights are a set of entitlements for all children, of whatever age and background. Most children's rights advocates use the UN Convention on the Rights of the Child (CRC) as their guide to children's human rights. This international human rights treaty took 10 years to develop. The CRC grants children in all parts of the world a comprehensive set of economic, social and cultural and civil and political rights.

Children, like adults, must respect the rights of others

What are the basic beliefs behind children's rights?

Children's rights advocates believe that children's and young people's lives are important and valid NOW. We do not think that children's worth rests on the fact that they will one day become adults. We see that children and young people are discriminated against as a group, and we are committed to working with them to make major improvements in their lives and status. Children's rights advocates believe strongly that children and young people should always have a say when decisions are being made that affect them, either as individuals or as a group. Often it will be necessary for children and young people to have support from independent advocates to help them express their views and ideas. Some people often mistakenly believe that children's rights are all about children and young people acting irrespons-

Children's Rights Alliance
for England

ibly with no thought for others. Another common misconception is that children's rights deprive children of their childhood. Human rights treaties, including the CRC, never give human beings unfettered rights: children, like adults, must respect the rights of others. In addition, there is no need to be concerned about children being robbed of their childhood: the CRC was designed completely around children's lives and needs and includes, for example, the right to play and the right to education.

Can children have rights without responsibilities?

Children and young people do have responsibilities: many have jobs, some care for relatives, a large proportion are school or college students, and they all must respect other people's rights and act within the law. However, human rights are not conditional on behaviour or responsibilities, though everyone has a responsibility to respect and uphold the human rights of others.

How old do children have to be before their views must be listened to?

The UN Convention on the Rights of the Child (CRC), which has the status of international law, does not give a minimum age for when children must be listened to. Article 12 of the CRC states that 'any child who is capable of forming his or her views [has] the right to express those views freely in all matters affecting them'. Research shows that very young children can form and express a view on extremely complex matters such as medical care and treatment.

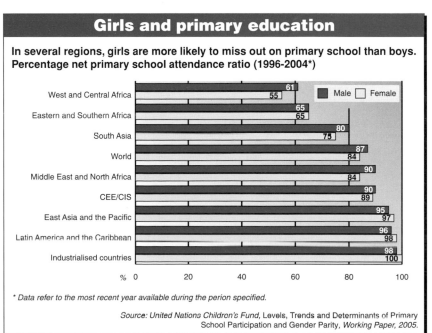

Girls and primary education

In several regions, girls are more likely to miss out on primary school than boys. Percentage net primary school attendance ratio (1996-2004*)

Region	Male	Female
West and Central Africa	61	55
Eastern and Southern Africa	65	65
South Asia	80	75
World	87	84
Middle East and North Africa	90	84
CEE/CIS	90	89
East Asia and the Pacific	95	97
Latin America and the Caribbean	96	98
Industrialised countries	98	100

% 0   20   40   60   80   100

* Data refer to the most recent year available during the perion specified.

Source: United Nations Children's Fund, Levels, Trends and Determinants of Primary School Participation and Gender Parity, Working Paper, 2005.

See, for example, *Children's consent to surgery* by Priscilla Alderson (Open University Press, 1993).

Can children go to court if their rights are breached?

Children and young people are not able to go to court if their rights under the UN Convention on the Rights of the Child are breached. However, children and young people can use the courts if their rights under UK law are violated. This includes civil and political rights protected by the Human Rights Act 1998; rights under education, health and social care law; and sex, race and disability equality legislation. Children and young people can also bring a case to the European Court of Human Rights in Strasbourg, France.

Isn't there a risk that emphasising rights will encourage children to disrespect adults?

Promoting children's and young people's human rights encourages mutual respect and positive behaviour. A commitment to children's human rights shows that adults respect children and young people, and take them seriously as individual people. This can only make relationships better, not worse.

Isn't it better to talk about children's needs rather than children's rights?

Children's human rights are based on their needs. An emphasis on rights rather than needs shows a commitment to seeing and respecting children and young people as citizens who have justified claims on society.

The UN Convention on the Rights of the Child (CRC) is clear that parents have the first responsibility to meet children's needs but that, if parents cannot meet their responsibilities, then society and the state must shoulder them. All political creeds and parties recognise that children have the right to have their needs met. Definitions of what children need are subject to professional and political judgement, yet children's human rights as expressed by the CRC are clear and universal: they apply to all children. It took 10 years for the United Nations to prepare the CRC as a comprehensive statement of what children across the globe require to achieve their fullest potential.

As soon as children are able to make informed judgements about cultural and religious matters, they have the right to exercise that choice

---

What happens when children's rights clash with cultural or religious traditions?

The UN Convention on the Rights of the Child (CRC) stresses the role of parents in looking after, guiding and supporting children, according to children's 'evolving capacities'. This means that as soon as children are able to make informed judgements about cultural and religious matters, they have the right to exercise choice. Some aspects of cultural or religious traditions have a lasting impact on children and young people – genital mutilation for example. In these circumstances, decisions should never be taken until children and young people are able to exercise an informed and free choice.

How well does our country respect children's human rights

The Committee on the Rights of the Child monitors how well governments uphold children's human rights. In October 2002 it issued a very critical report on the UK, with 78 recommendations for action on children's rights. Every year, CRAE reviews Government action on these 78 recommendations – in November 2004, we published a report showing there had been significant progress in only 17 areas.

Is there an age limit for when children and young people can instruct solicitors?

There is no lower age limit for children instructing solicitors but they have to demonstrate that they understand the processes involved. In criminal matters, children are seen to be competent to instruct solicitors from the age of 10 years.

Is there anyone in the Government who has special responsibility to promote and protect children's human rights?

The Children, Young People and Families Directorate in the Department for Education and Skills has special responsibility for the UN Convention on the Rights of the Child in England. The Minister responsible is Beverley Hughes MP. The Foreign and Commonwealth Office and the Department for International Development seek to promote children's human rights internationally. The FCO has, since 1998, published an annual human rights report.

■ Information from the Children's Rights Alliance for England. Visit www.crae.org.uk for more information.

© CRAE

Children's rights timeline

Information from UNICEF

20 November 1989

Convention on the Rights of the Child adopted by the United Nations

The Convention spells out children's rights and asks countries to protect these rights. These rights include education, protection, health care and survival. By 2002, almost every country in the world had ratified the Convention.

8 September 2000

Millennium Declaration adopted Millennium Development Goals

The Millennium Declaration is a commitment to development, peace and human rights. Nearly 200 leaders have adopted the Declaration, and committed themselves to achieving eight development goals with specific targets by 2015.

> *The Convention on the Rights of the Child spells out children's rights and asks countries to protect these rights. These rights include education, protection, health care and survival*

29-30 September 2000

World Summit for Children World Declaration on the Survival, Protection and Development of Children

Governments met at the United Nations to agree on what actions, goals and promises need to be taken to make sure children are healthy, educated and protected from war and exploitation. They agree to review their progress in 10 years at a special session for children.

April 2001

Say Yes for Children Campaign

The Global Movement for Children begins mobilising every citizen of every nation to change the world with children. The Say Yes for Children campaign builds on this momentum, with millions of child-ren and adults around the world pledging their support for critical actions to improve children's lives.

May 2001

UN Secretary General issues Report on progress for children We the Children

The United Nations Secretary-General issues a report on progress made for children since the World Summit. In this report, the Secretary-General notes both the world's greatest achievements of the decade, and where there is still 'room for improvement'.

5-7 May 2002

Children's Forum A World Fit for Us

More than 400 child delegates to the United Nations Special Session on Children prepared for their participation at the Special Session. They discussed the many issues facing children today and ways young people can work with world leaders to make a difference in the lives of children everywhere.

8-10 May 2002

Special Session on Children A World Fit for Children

A follow-up to the World Summit for Children, governments, world leaders, business people, NGOs and children looked at the progress made since 1990 and agreed on the next steps to take to create a better world fit for children.

■ The above information is re-printed with kind permission from UNICEF. For more infromation, please visit their website at www. unicef.org.uk.

© UNICEF

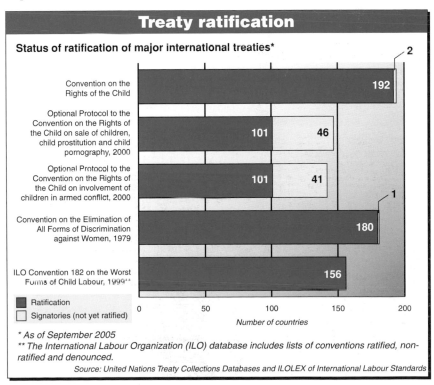

Treaty ratification

Status of ratification of major international treaties*

Treaty	Ratification	Signatories (not yet ratified)
Convention on the Rights of the Child	192	2
Optional Protocol to the Convention on the Rights of the Child on sale of children, child prostitution and child pornography, 2000	101	46
Optional Protocol to the Convention on the Rights of the Child on involvement of children in armed conflict, 2000	101	41
Convention on the Elimination of All Forms of Discrimination against Women, 1979	180	1
ILO Convention 182 on the Worst Forms of Child Labour, 1999**	156	

■ Ratification
□ Signatories (not yet ratified)

Number of countries

* As of September 2005
** The International Labour Organization (ILO) database includes lists of conventions ratified, non-ratified and denounced.

Source: United Nations Treaty Collections Databases and ILOLEX of International Labour Standards

Convention on the Rights of the Child

Frequently asked questions

What is the Convention on the Rights of the Child?

The Convention on the Rights of the Child is an international treaty that recognises the human rights of children, defined as persons up to the age of 18 years. The Convention establishes in international law that State Parties must ensure that all children – without discrimination in any form – benefit from special protection measures and assistance; have access to services such as education and health care; can develop their personalities, abilities and talents to the fullest potential; grow up in an environment of happiness, love and understanding; and are informed about and participate in achieving their rights in an accessible and active manner.

How was it decided what should go into the Convention on the Rights of the Child?

The standards in the Convention on the Rights of the Child were negotiated by governments, non-governmental organisations, human rights advocates, lawyers, health specialists, social workers, educators, child development experts and religious leaders from all over the world, over a 10-year period. The result is a consensus document that takes into account the importance of tradition and cultural values for the protection and harmonious development of the child. It reflects the principal legal systems of the world and acknowledges the specific needs of developing countries.

How does the Convention on the Rights of the Child protect children's rights?

It constitutes a common reference against which progress in meeting human rights standards for children can be assessed and results compared. Having agreed to meet the standards in the Convention, governments are obliged to bring their legislation, policy and practice into accordance with the standards in the Convention; to transform the standards into reality for all children; and to abstain from any action that may preclude the enjoyment of those rights or violate them. Governments are required to report periodically to a committee of independent experts on their progress to achieve all the rights.

How does the international community monitor and support progress on the implementation of the Convention?

The Committee on the Rights of the Child, an internationally elected body of independent experts that sits in Geneva to monitor the Convention's implementation, requires governments that have ratified the Convention to submit regular reports on the status of children's rights in their countries. The Committee reviews and comments on these reports and encourages States to take special measures and to develop special institutions for the promotion and protection of children's rights. Where necessary, the Committee calls for international assistance from other governments and technical assistance from organizations like UNICEF. For more information, see the 'Implementation' page under 'Using the Convention for Children' on the UNICEF website.

How is the Convention special?

The Convention:
- Is in force in virtually the entire community of nations, thus providing a common ethical and legal framework to develop an agenda for children. At the same time, it constitutes a common reference against which progress may be assessed.
- Was the first time a formal commitment was made to ensure the realisation of human rights and monitor progress on the situation of children.
- Indicates that children's rights are human rights. Children's rights are not special rights, but rather the fundamental rights inherent to the human dignity of all people, including children. Children's rights can no longer be perceived

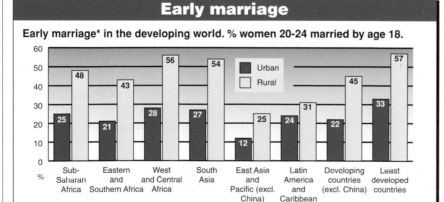

Early marriage

Early marriage* in the developing world. % women 20-24 married by age 18.

Legend: Urban, Rural

Sub-Saharan Africa: 25, 48
Eastern and Southern Africa: 21, 43
West and Central Africa: 28, 56
South Asia: 27, 54
East Asia and Pacific (excl. China): 12, 25
Latin America and Caribbean: 24, 31
Developing countries (excl. China): 22, 45
Least developed countries: 33, 57

* Early marriage: Percentage of women aged 20-24 that were married or in statutory or customary union recognised as marriage before they were 18 years old.
Regional averages: These aggregates do not include all countries in each region. However, sufficient data were available for more than 50% of the target population to generate the averages for the regions shown.
Data range: Data refer to the most recent year available during the period specified.

Source: Multiple Indicator Cluster Surveys (MICS), Demographic and Health Surveys (DHS) and other national surveys.

as an option, as a question of favour or kindness to children or as an expression of charity. They generate obligations and responsibilities that we all must honour and respect.

- Was even accepted by non-state entities. The Sudan People's Liberation Army (SPLA), a rebel movement in Southern Sudan, is one such example.
- Is a reference for many organisations working with and for children – including NGOs and organisations within the UN system.
- Reaffirms that all rights are important and essential for the full development of the child and that addressing each and every child is important.
- Reaffirms the notion of State accountability for the realisation of human rights and the values of transparency and public scrutiny that are associated with it.

- Promotes an international system of solidarity designed to achieve the realisation of children's rights. Using the Convention's reporting process as a reference, donor countries are required to provide assistance in areas where particular needs have been identified; recipient countries are required to direct overseas development assistance (ODA) to that end too.
- Highlights and defends the family's role in children's lives.

How does the Convention on the Rights of the Child define a child?

The Convention defines a 'child' as a person below the age of 18, unless the relevant laws recognise an earlier age of majority. In some cases, States are obliged to be consistent in defining benchmark ages – such as the age for admission into employment and completion of compulsory education; but in other cases the Convention is unequivocal in setting an upper limit – such as prohibiting life imprisonment or capital punishment for those under 18 years of age.

How many countries have ratified the Convention on the Rights of the Child?

More countries have ratified the Convention than any other human rights treaty in history – 192 countries had become State Parties to the Convention as of November 2005.

More countries have ratified the Convention than any other human rights treaty in history

---

Who has not ratified the Convention on the Rights of the Child and why?

The Convention on the Rights of the Child is the most widely and rapidly ratified human rights treaty in history. Only two countries, Somalia and the United States, have not ratified this celebrated agreement. Somalia is currently unable to proceed to ratification as it has no recognised government. By signing the Convention, the United States has signalled its intention to ratify – but has yet to do so.

As in many other nations, the United States undertakes an extensive examination and scrutiny of treaties before proceeding to ratify. This examination, which includes an evaluation of the degree of compliance with existing law and practice in the country at state and federal levels, can take several years – or even longer if the treaty is portrayed as being controversial or if

the process is politicised. Moreover, the US Government typically will consider only one human rights treaty at a time. Currently, the Convention on the Elimination of All Forms of Discrimination against Women is cited as the nation's top priority among human rights treaties.

How does UNICEF use the Convention on the Rights of the Child?

The Secretary-General of the United Nations has called for the mainstreaming of human rights in all areas of UN operations – for example, the Office of the United Nations High Commissioner for Refugees (UNHCR) in its mandate for refugee children, or the International Labour Organization (ILO) in its commitment to eliminate child labour. In the case of UNICEF, the Convention has become more than just a reference, but a systematic guide to the work of the organization. As expressed in its Mission Statement, UNICEF is mandated to 'advocate for the protection of children's rights' and it 'strives to establish children's rights as enduring ethical principles and international standards of behaviour towards children'. UNICEF promotes the principles and provisions of the Convention and the mainstreaming of children's rights in a systematic manner, in its advocacy, programming, monitoring and evaluation activities.

The Convention on the Rights of the Child provides UNICEF with guidance as to the areas to be assessed and addressed, and it is a tool against which UNICEF measures the progress achieved in those areas. Integrating a human rights approach in all UNICEF's work is an ongoing learning process that includes broadening the framework for UNICEF's development agenda. In addition to maintaining a focus on child survival and development, UNICEF must consider the situation of all children, better analyse the economic and social environment, develop partnerships to strengthen the response (including the participation of children themselves), support interventions on the basis of non-discrimination and act in the best interests of the child.

CONVENTION ON THE RIGHTS OF THE CHILD

What steps do the Convention on the Rights of the Child and the Committee on the Rights of the Child encourage governments to undertake?

Through its reviews of country reports, the Committee urges all levels of government to use the Convention as a guide in policy-making and implementation to:

■ Develop a comprehensive national agenda for children.

■ Develop permanent bodies or mechanisms to promote co-ordination, monitoring and evaluation of activities throughout all sectors of government.

■ Ensure that all legislation is fully compatible with the Convention.

■ Make children visible in policy development processes throughout government by introducing child impact assessments.

■ Carry out adequate budget analysis to determine the portion of public funds spent on children and to ensure that these resources are being used effectively.

■ Ensure that sufficient data are collected and used to improve the plight of all children in each jurisdiction.

■ Raise awareness and disseminate information on the Convention by providing training to all those involved in government policy-making and working with or for children.

■ Involve civil society – including children themselves – in the process of implementing and raising awareness of child rights.

■ Set up independent statutory offices – ombudspersons, commissions and other institutions – to promote children's rights.

In addition to support of country programmes, how does UNICEF assist governments in promoting children's rights?

UNICEF's work involves advocacy, cooperation and technical assistance.

■ UNICEF undertakes advocacy – through publications, awareness campaigns and participation in major international conferences and in public statements – and works with those responsible for the development and implementation of legislation and public policy.

■ UNICEF cooperates with both donor governments and governments in the developing world. UNICEF-assisted programmes seek to ensure the social and economic rights of children by delivering essential services such as health and education and improving access to good nutrition and to care. UNICEF also focuses attention on national budget spending, encouraging governments to allocate 20 per cent of budgets to basic services. Further, UNICEF supports efforts to redress inequitable practices and discrimination, which are direct and underlying causes of children's and women's deprivation.

■ UNICEF cooperates with other international organisations – particularly those within the UN system, as the United Nations Development Assistance Framework (UNDAF) process illustrates – and international financial institutions.

■ UNICEF works to build partnerships with civil society organisations, involving children, families and other members of communities.

■ UNICEF provides technical support and assistance to the Committee on the Rights of the Child.

■ UNICEF focuses on sustainable results and encourages ongoing monitoring and evaluation of programmes.

What are some of the areas in which the Convention on the Rights of the Child has been most effective?

The Convention has inspired a process of national implementation and social change in all regions of the world, including:

■ Incorporating human rights principles into legislation;

■ Establishing interdepartmental and multidisciplinary bodies;

■ Developing national agendas for children;

■ Widening partnerships for children;

■ Promoting ombudspersons for children or commissioners for children's rights;

■ Assessing the impact of measures on children;

■ Restructuring of budgetary allocations;

■ Targeting child survival and development;

■ Implementing the principle of non-discrimination;

■ Listening to children's voices; and

■ Developing justice systems for children.

These examples are merely a sampling and are not exhaustive. For more information and further country-specific examples, see the 'National Implementation' fact sheet within Resources on the UNICEF website.

■ Information from UNICEF. Visit www.unicef.org.uk for more.

© UNICEF

Excluded from democratic debate

Young people and the right to vote

Louise King, Senior Policy Officer at the Children's Rights Alliance for England (CRAE), argues that the voting age should be lowered to 16.

16- and 17-year-olds can work and pay taxes, be a company director, serve a custodial sentence, raise children and get married but somehow they are not considered responsible enough to vote.

There are one and a half million 16- and 17-year-olds in this country, yet how often do we hear senior politicians saying anything positive about them?

The prevailing discourse on children and young people is youth crime and anti-social behaviour: Tony Blair's 'respect agenda' aims to deal with 'out of control kids' and young people 'causing a nuisance in their local community'. The recently launched *Youth Matters* is a Green Paper for the deserving teenager: those who misbehave will not get top-ups on their new 'opportunity card', or they may have their card withdrawn altogether. This is at a time when recorded offending by children and young people has been in decline for several years.

The truth is that senior politicians have no incentive to advocate for children and young people or to raise awareness among adult communities of children's and young people's concerns and experiences. This is a group of people that has very little political power. They are the subject of many focus group discussions, especially on anti-social behaviour, yet they rarely get to sit round the table. No vote, no value.

Fortunately, change may be on the way. The Electoral Reform Bill, expected in the autumn, offers an excellent opportunity to amend the law to give 16- and 17-year-olds the vote. The Children's Rights Alliance for England (CRAE) will be energetically lobbying to ensure this opportunity is not wasted. CRAE is a coalition of over 280 voluntary and statutory organisations committed to the fullest implementation of the Convention on the Rights of the Child. CRAE is especially concerned that children and young people get the chance to participate in all decisons that affect them.

Convention on the Rights of the Child

In November 1989, the United Nations adopted the UN Convention on the Rights of the Child (CRC). Taking 10 years to develop, the CRC gives all under-18-year-olds a comprehensive set of rights, including article 12 which gives children and young people the right to have their views taken into account in all matters that affect them. The UK ratified the CRC in 1991.

In Ocotber 2002, the international monitoring body for the Convention on the Rights of the Child – the Committee on the Rights of the Child issued its concluding observations on the UK. These set out the Committee's analysis of the state of children's rights in the UK, and give recommendations on how children's rights can be fully realised. In relation to children's and young people's participation rights, the Committee recommended that 'the State party take further steps to consistently reflect the obligations of both paragraphs of article 12 in legislation'.

The right to vote is also an inalienable human right enshrined in Article 3 of the First Protocol of the European Convention on Human Rights (ECHR) and article 25 of the International Covenant on Civil and Political Rights (ICCPR):

- Article 3 of the First Protocol of the ECHR guarantees free, secret elections, at reasonable intervals, which ensure the free expression of the opinion of the people in the choice of the legislator. Article 2 provides for non-discrimination in the application of ECHR rights.
- Article 25 of ICCPR gives every citizen the right and the opportunity, without distinctions and without unreasonable restrictions, to vote.

In March last year (2004), in a case brought by life-sentenced prisoner John Hirst, the European Court of Human Rights ruled that banning prisoners from voting breached Article 3 of the First Protocol of the ECHR. The UK government's appeal against the ruling was heard in April 2004 and the final decision is expected in Ocotber. CRAE will be looking carefully at the final decision to see what implications it has on the exclusion from voting of 16- and 17-year-olds.

Rich and varied lives

Many people question whether 16-year-olds are responsible enough to vote. This shows just how excluded and disrespected young people are. 16- and 17-year-olds have considerable responsibilities, and routinely make complex decisions, for example, 650,000 16- and 17-year-olds are in employment and 61,000 16- and 17-year-olds are the main carer of a sick or disabled relative.

Addtionally at 16 and 17 years of age, young people:

- Will have spent at least 11 years in school

- Are legally permitted to leave home
- Can have sexual relationships
- Can consent to medical treatment
- Can buy cigarettes
- Can get married (with parental consent in England and Wales; without parental consent in Scotland)
- Can change their name by deed poll
- Have to pay for prescriptions, dental treatment or eyesight tests (unless in full-time education, or receiving social security benefits)
- Have to pay full fare on public transport
- Can leave local authority care
- Can claim social security benefits in certain circumstances.

At 17 years of age, they can:
- Join the armed forces (with parental consent if female)
- Pilot a plane or helicopter
- Be interviewed by police without the presence of an 'appropriate adult'.

The lives of 16- and 17-year-olds are as rich and varied as at any other age and research has shown that young people's attitudes are very similar to older people's (J Holland and R Thompson, 1999). Young people care about the same things as adults – health, education and crime (British Youth Council, 2000).

Moreoverm if adult voters always act so responsibly when voting, then why do wet polling days seem to favour the Conservative Party? Why has research shown that voters are more likely to choose a candidate at the top of their ballot paper? And why did the state of California elect someone better known for his movie star status than political credentials?

The arguments used against women being given the vote in the early part of the 20th century seem ridiculous in 2005: women were seen as too innocent and naive for the world of politics; and it was argued that their husbands knew what was in their best interests. Sound familiar?

Young people want to vote at 16

One of the arguments against extending the franchise put forward by government in the past is that there is no real push for this from young people. This is likely to be more a symptom of how excluded young people are from traditional political processes, than a sign that young people are happy with the status quo. Unless we actively engage with young people to find out their views, we are in no position to say what concerns them.

Last year, the Electoral Commission published a report that recommended the voting age stay at 18 years. It concluded from its research (which included a poll of just 234 young people) that a majority of young people do not want the voting age reduced. By contrast a wealth of research – with much larger groups of young people – has consistently shown support for votes at 16:
- The Yvote/Ynot? Project in 2002, which consulted with more than 1,500 young people (DfES 2002)
- The British Youth Council consultation for the European youth white paper (British Youth Council 2002)
- Save the Children UK consultation with over 500 under-18s in England in 1999 (SCFUK 1999)
- A Children's Society research project carried out in 1999.

Organisations run by and for young people have been campaigning for many years for the voting age to be reduced to 16: the British Youth Council has campaigned for two decades, the UK Youth Parliament since its establishment in 2000 and Article 12 since 1999.

These are not new arguments. Historical sources from the early part of the last century indicate that, prior to female suffrage, those opposed to women getting the vote argued that a significant number of women did not want it. Nevertheless, history shows it was the right thing to do: how many women today would not want the right to vote?

Polls have found, unsurprisingly, that the majority of adults do not support an extension of the franchise, though attitudes are slowly changing. While we welcome growing public support for votes at 16, we do not believe that overwhelming public support should be the prerequisite for extending the vote.

In 1969, public opinion polls showed that a majority of the public did not support reducing the voting age to 18 years. Parliament was right to press ahead with reform, as it had done decades earlier with women's suffrage.

Further information

CRAE has recently launched a comprehensive set of participation training materials called Ready Steady Change. For more information about this, the votes at 16 campaign or the other work of CRAE, please visit www.crae.org.uk or telephone 020 7278 8222.

- The above information is an extract from the British Institute of Human Rights' Autumn 2005 newsletter. Visit www.bihr.org for more information.

© BIHR

The right to participation

Information from UNICEF

Several provisions in the Convention on the Rights of the Child reflect children's right to participation. Participation is one of the guiding principles of the Convention, as well as one of its basic challenges. Article 12 of the Convention on the Rights of the Child states that children have the right to participate in decision-making processes that may be relevant in their lives and to influence decisions taken in their regard – within the family, the school or the community. The principle affirms that children are full-fledged persons who have the right to express their views in all matters affecting them and requires that those views be heard and given due weight in accordance with the child's age and maturity. It recognises the potential of children to enrich decision-making processes, to share perspectives and to participate as citizens and actors of change. The practical meaning of children's right to participation must be considered in each and every matter concerning children.

As a fundamental right of the child, the right to participation stands on its own; it requires a clear commitment and effective actions to become a living reality and therefore is much more than a simple strategy. It was for this reason that the Committee on the Rights of the Child identified the right to participation as one of the guiding principles of the Convention. Participation is an underlying value that needs to guide the way each individual right is ensured and respected; a criterion to assess progress in the implementation process of children's rights; and an additional dimension to the universally recognised freedom of expression, implying the right of the child to be heard and to have his or her views or opinions taken into account.

> **Article 12 of the Convention on the Rights of the Child states that children have the right to participate in decision-making processes that may be relevant in their lives**

Respecting children's views means that such views should not be ignored; it does not mean that children's opinions should be automatically endorsed. Expressing an opinion is not the same as taking a decision, but it implies the ability to influence decisions. A process of dialogue and exchange needs to be encouraged in which children assume increasing responsibilities and become active, tolerant and democratic. In such a process, adults must provide direction and guidance to children while considering their views in a manner consistent with the child's age and maturity. Through this process, the child will gain an understanding of why particular options are followed, or why decisions are taken that might differ from the one he or she favoured.

Free from pressure and manipulation

The child's participation is a right and children therefore are free to express their views or, if they prefer, to not do so. Children should not be pressured, constrained or influenced in ways that might prevent them from freely expressing their opinions or leave them feeling manipulated. This principle clearly applies in some judicial proceedings, in which a child is forced to participate as a witness even if the legal outcome may contravene the child's best interests.

In many countries, children are expected to join judicial proceedings as witnesses yet are rarely entitled to

directly launch complaints as victims – even in cases where the child has been ill-treated or sexually abused. Such laws often foresee the possibility of parents or caregivers launching the complaint on behalf of the child – which of course does not address situations in which a child is a victim within his or her own family.

Children's evolving capacity

The Convention sets no minimum age at which children can begin expressing their views freely, nor does it limit the contexts in which children can express their views. The Convention acknowledges that children can and do form views from a very early age and refers to children's 'evolving capacity' for decision-making. This means, for example, that parents and, where appropriate, members of the family and wider community are expected to give appropriate direction, guidance or advice to children. But parents' guidance and advice takes on greater value and meaning as children grow and develop, gain maturity and experience, become more autonomous and more responsible.

In a manner consistent with the child's age and maturity, there will be various ways of creating the right atmosphere to enable the child to freely express his or her views. Within age groups, the ability, confidence and experience of the individual child in assessing his or her own situation, considering possible options, expressing views and influencing decision-making processes will all have a bearing on how such an atmosphere can be achieved.

The Convention sets no minimum age at which children can begin expressing their views freely, nor does it limit the contexts in which children can express their views

---

Among children, it is important that the older and more advantaged foster the participation of the younger and most disadvantaged, including girls, the poorest, children belonging to minority and indigenous groups and migrant children.

The role of parents and others

The child's evolving capacity represents just one side of the equation: the other involves adults' evolving capacity and willingness to listen to and learn from their children, to understand and consider the child's point of view, to be willing to re-examine their own opinions and attitudes and to envisage solutions that address children's views. For adults, as well as for children, participation is a challenging learning process and cannot be reduced to a simple formality. Fulfilling the right of children to participate entails training and mobilising adults who live and work with children, so that they are prepared to give children the chance to freely and increasingly participate in society and gain democratic skills. Parents and other family members are most obviously included in this group, as well as teachers, social workers, lawyers, psychologists, the police and other members of the society at large.

Ensuring appropriate information

As mentioned earlier, children's right to participation as outlined in article 12 is closely linked to freedom of expression. It is also related to fulfilling the right to information, a key prerequisite for children's participation to be relevant and meaningful. It is in fact essential that children be provided with the necessary information about options that exist and the consequences of such options so that they can make informed and free decisions. Providing information enables children to gain skills, confidence and maturity in expressing views and influencing decisions.

Article 15 states that children have the right to create and join associations and to assemble peacefully. Both imply opportunities to

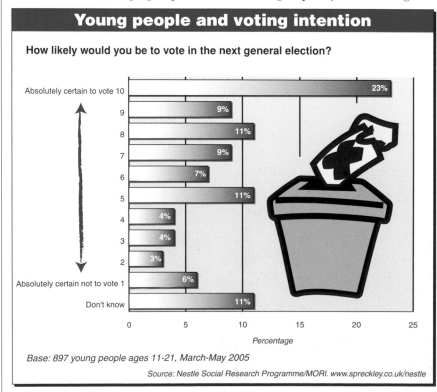

Young people and voting intention

How likely would you be to vote in the next general election?

	Percentage
Absolutely certain to vote 10	23%
9	9%
8	11%
7	9%
6	7%
5	11%
4	4%
3	4%
2	3%
Absolutely certain not to vote 1	6%
Don't know	11%

Base: 897 young people ages 11-21, March-May 2005

Source: Nestle Social Research Programme/MORI. www.spreckley.co.uk/nestle

express political opinions, engage in political processes and participate in decision-making. Both are critical to the development of a democratic society and to the participation of children in the realisation of their rights.

Participation is the path to other rights

The right to participation is relevant to the exercise of all other rights, within the family, the school and the larger community context. Thus, for example:

- **Adoption.** As one of 'the persons concerned', the child should be heard in any judicial or administrative adoption proceedings. Article 21(a) refers to the informed consent of persons concerned, including the child.
- **Separation from parents.** In decisions to be taken on the need to separate a child from his or her parents (for example, on the basis of abuse or neglect), the child – as an 'interested party' – must be given an opportunity to participate and make his or her views known.
- **Name change.** In a decision to be taken on the changing of a child's name, the views of the child should be taken into consideration.
- **Right to health.** Children are entitled to be informed, have access to information and be supported in the use of basic knowledge of child health and nutrition (article 24(2)e) so that they may enjoy their right to health.
- **Education.** Children's participation takes on a special dimension in the area of education. Education should

give children the opportunity to develop their talents and abilities to full potential, to gain confidence and self-esteem, to use their initiative and creativity, to gain life skills and take informed decisions and to understand and experience pluralism, tolerance and democratic coexistence. In brief, the right to education means the right to experience citizenship. To achieve citizenship and all it entails, children must be perceived not as mere recipients of knowledge, but rather as active players in the learning process. It is for this reason that the Convention puts so much emphasis on the aims of education (article 28) and on an educational system that respects the child's human dignity.

Participation cannot be genuine if children have no opportunity to understand the consequences and the impact of their opinions

---

Genuine participation versus tokenism

Participation cannot be genuine if children have no opportunity to understand the consequences and the impact of their opinions – such non-genuine 'participation' often merely disguises what is actually the manipulation of children, or

tokenism. Again, the key to genuine participation is ensuring respect for children's views. In addition to facilitating and supporting activities to foster child participation, it is becoming increasingly important to consider whether and how to ensure follow-up of children's recommendations and concerns.

Children's referendums and the 'What do you think?' project are but a few examples of a worldwide movement to increase the spaces and opportunities for child participation. In all such activities, strong monitoring and evaluation components must be present and initiatives

tested against the principles of the Convention. Is the activity in the best interests of the child? Is any form of discrimination present? Do the most disadvantaged and marginalised children have opportunities to participate and are their voices heard? Are children genuinely participating? Can children make a difference in decision-making processes?

- The above information is reprinted with kind permission from UNICEF. Visit www.unicef.org.uk for more information.

Children's groups warn punishment not a panacea

By Polly Curtis and Rosie Cowan

The government's respect agenda risks alienating vulnerable youngsters and breaching their human rights, children's rights campaigners warned last night.

Among the critics of the plans is the children's commissioner, Al Aynsley Green, who told the *Guardian* he was 'concerned about a knee-jerk reaction and a one-size-fits all response where punishment is the answer'. 'I would remind the government that children's rights are protected by the UN Convention on Human Rights,' he said. They are entitled to the right to meet in public, to privacy and to have a say in the decisions affecting their lives, he added.

Bob Reitemeier, chief executive of the Children's Society, said: 'The effects of the government's existing policies, such as Asbos, dispersal powers and curfews, have made many young people feel demonised, disrespected and alienated within their communities.'

The prime minister's offer to support families has also caused some confusion. Heads of social services warned that the £70m earmarked for parenting support programmes through local authorities was dwarfed by a £600m funding shortfall in children's services over the next financial year.

Andrew Webb, co-chair of the association of directors of social services' children and families committee, said: 'We don't have enough money, we can't take it out of schools or the care system, so the only place that's left is preventative support for families.

'At the same time the prime minister is saying we ought to be doing more to support parents to prevent antisocial behaviour. That's our dilemma.'

Chris Stanley of the crime reduction charity Nacro warned against replacing established programmes to support families with untested schemes. 'Although establishing a national parenting academy may sound impressive in theory, more money needs to be invested into schemes that we know are really making a difference to individuals, families and communities,' he said.

However, the action plan was welcomed by the London mayor, Ken Livingstone, and Sir Ian Blair, the Scotland Yard commissioner, as they showed off the city's Safer Neighbourhood policing scheme to the Los Angeles police chief, Bill Bratton, on a walkabout in Camden yesterday morning.

'You've got to take the streets back before you build a respect agenda,' said Mr Livingstone. 'If you discourage kids from getting into that first bit of bother, it stops them becoming involved in criminal activity down the line.'

Mr Bratton, the former New York police chief famed for his zero tolerance to minor crime, compared Tony Blair's move to what the then mayor of New York, Rudolph Giuliani, achieved in the 1990s.

Sir Ian said: 'The decision by the police authority, the Met and the mayor to go down this route [neighbourhood policing] is part of the building of what the prime minister has launched, to be the vibrant society London needs to be by the time the Olympics arrive.'

11 January 2006

© Guardian Newspapers Limited 2006

Youth justice – the facts

Information from Barnardo's

- over 50% of children in custody have been in care.
- 70% have suffered abuse.
- 90% have mental-health problems.
- custody alone does not discourage further offending.
- the time delay between a young person being charged with an offence and a court appearance reduces the young person's sense of responsibility and provides opportunity for further offending.
- up to 90% of young men commit a crime of some kind, although the number of young people committing serious crime is relatively small.
- 88% of those who receive custodial sentences reoffended within two years of leaving custody.
- Britain imprisons more young people than almost any other country in Europe – despite the fact that there is no corresponding increase in serious youth crime.
- between 1992 and 1999 custodial sentences for children and young people rose by 90%.
- on release from prison 80% of young people will reoffend.
- the increase in the use of custody for children puts the UK government in breach of Article 37 of the UN Convention on the Rights of the Child, which states that the imprisonment of children should be used only as a last resort.

- The above information is reprinted with kind permission from Barnardo's. Visit www.barnardos.org.uk for more information.

© Barnardo's

I'm a teenager, what happened to my rights?

Executive summary

The UN Convention on the Rights of the Child (CRC) was ratified on 20 November 1989 and has now been part of international law for 15 years. Yet many children who have grown up within the lifetime of the CRC have now reached their teenage years knowing little or nothing of what it is to have the protection and freedoms enshrined within its 54 articles.

As this cohort of children reach their teenage years they face a new range of threats to their rights and wellbeing. Adolescents under the age of 18 are still children, and as such they are entitled to the protections offered by the CRC. But all too often teenagers are mistaken for, or treated as adults. Millions of teenagers in the developing world must grow up fast and take on roles and responsibilities far beyond their physical and emotional capacity. Millions of young girls become wives and mothers whilst they are still children. In Andhra Pradesh, India, the mean age for marriage for girls in rural areas is just 14.7 and studies reveal that between 20 and 30 per cent of girls in India give birth by the time they are 17.

As a result of the AIDS pandemic more and more adolescents of both genders are taking on the role of carers to sick relatives and/or becoming breadwinners. Economic necessity means teenage children are often forced to work to support themselves and their families. It is estimated that between 100 and 150 million children live on the street, the majority of whom are adolescents. In sub-Saharan Africa AIDS has orphaned an estimated 12.3 million children, and this number is set to rise to 25 million by 2010. As a result more and more teenagers are having to take on the role of parents and breadwinners for their younger siblings.

It is likely that the majority of teenagers born on the day the CRC was ratified have not benefited from the promises it contains and know nothing about the rights it affords them.

Children who survive the dangers of early childhood face new health risks as they enter their teenage years. They risk becoming infected with HIV/AIDS and other sexually transmitted diseases. In some parts of Africa there is a widespread belief that HIV/AIDS can be cured by having sex with a virgin, but this is resulting in more and more teenage girls becoming infected. Teenage girls are becoming infected at five times the rate of teenage boys because of this practice as well as because of intergenerational marriage and relationships between older men and teenage girls.

Studies reveal that between 20 and 30 per cent of girls in India give birth by the time they are 17

Girls experiencing early pregnancy and childbirth risk severe complications or even death as a result of the stress on their immature bodies. Globally, girls aged 15-19 are twice as likely to die in childbirth as women in their twenties. And girls aged 10-14 are five times as likely to die. Save the Children estimates that 70,000 adolescent mothers die every year in the developing world because young girls are having children before they are physically ready for parenthood.

The social and economic pressures faced by teenagers lead many to resort to drug, alcohol, or substance abuse – often resulting in long-term addiction. Or they take health risks, such as smoking tobacco, that will affect their health in later life. In the US, the number of adolescents aged 12 to 17 receiving treatment for substance abuse rose

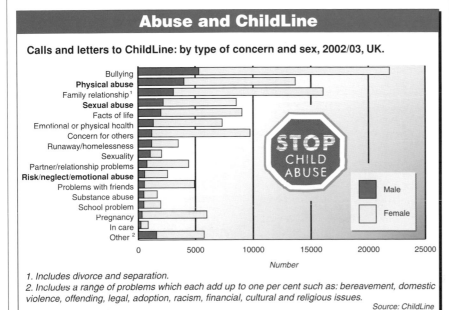

Abuse and ChildLine

Calls and letters to ChildLine: by type of concern and sex, 2002/03, UK.

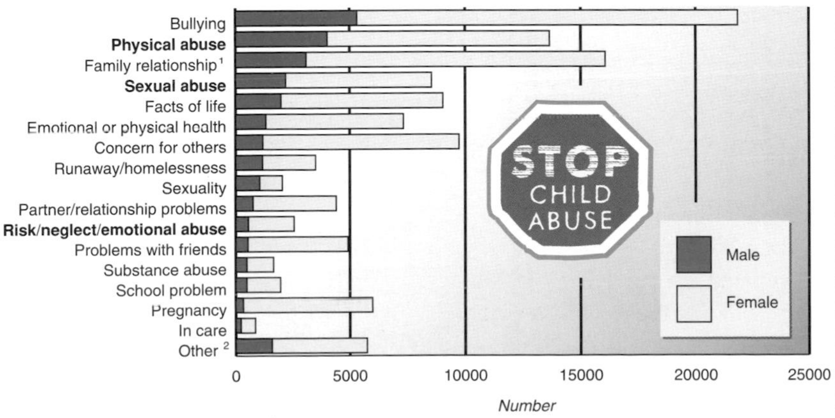
Bullying
Physical abuse
Family relationship¹
Sexual abuse
Facts of life
Emotional or physical health
Concern for others
Runaway/homelessness
Sexuality
Partner/relationship problems
Risk/neglect/emotional abuse
Problems with friends
Substance abuse
School problem
Pregnancy
In care
Other²
0
5000
10000
15000
20000
25000
Number
STOP
CHILD
ABUSE
Male
Female

1. Includes divorce and separation.
2. Includes a range of problems which each add up to one per cent such as: bereavement, domestic violence, offending, legal, adoption, racism, financial, cultural and religious issues.

Source: ChildLine

consistently from 1992 to 2002. In 1992, adolescents represented six per cent of all treatment admissions. By 2002, this proportion had grown to nine per cent.

As children grow up they become more independent from parents. But they are still naïve and inexperienced, and can find it hard to adjust to the transition stages as they approach adulthood. Researchers in the US have mapped the development of the brain from childhood to adulthood and found that it goes through profound changes during adolescence. The pace and magnitude of these changes show that the brain is still developing throughout the teenage years.

It is estimated that 246 million under-18s are engaged in child labour, and two-thirds of them – 171 million – are doing work that is hazardous

---

Many are recruited into organised crime, gang culture or dangerous employment. It is estimated that 246 million under-18s are engaged in child labour, and two-thirds of them – 171 million – are doing work that is hazardous, such as working with dangerous machinery or pesticides and chemicals. Children can be involved in child labour from a very young age but the older and stronger they become the more likely it is that they will be put to work. The most common type of work is agriculture, followed by domestic work.

Teenagers are targeted by traffickers, drug dealers, and recruiters looking for child soldiers. Between 8 million and 20 million children, the majority of whom are likely to be teenagers, are reported to be involved in the worst forms of child labour: forced and bonded labour, armed conflict, prostitution and pornography, and trafficking.

Millions of adolescents leave home – either voluntarily or because they have no option – and take to the streets where they are even more vulnerable. If they transgress the law, adolescents are often denied the special treatment accorded to younger children. Many experience brutality at the hands of the criminal justice system with numerous teenage children incarcerated in adult detention facilities. More than a million children and teenagers across the world are locked up, the majority of them under arrest or awaiting trial.

However, although adolescents below 18 are still children, they are grown-up enough to be listened to and have the right to voice their opinions and influence decisions affecting their lives. Teenagers are making their views known – and expecting adults to take notice of them. Plan facilitates teenagers to speak out through a range of media projects. As well as giving teenagers a platform to express themselves to a wide audience, these programmes provide training in broad non-vocational skills such as communication, teamwork, creativity, self-expression, and confidence. They also provide other children and teenagers as well as adults with information they would not otherwise receive and can influence change in their communities.

There is always hope for a better future. Children who are teenagers now can build a better future for themselves. And younger children can be afforded better protection when they reach adolescence. Positive things can and are being done to challenge the problems, not least by teenagers themselves. Teenagers are supporting themselves and their families. They are participating in educating their communities about children's rights, health – including HIV/AIDS – and non-violent solutions to conflict, to name but a few subjects. They are getting involved in community forums to influence decisions and bring about change for the better. Given the chance, teenagers are achieving their aspirations.

■ The above information is the executive summary of the report 'I'm a teenager, what happened to my rights?' and is reprinted with kind permission from Plan UK. For more information, please visit www.plan-uk.org.

© Plan UK

Human rights at school

Five-year-olds assert their 'human right' to be violent and unruly at school, says union

Children as young as five are asserting their 'human right' to do as they please as unruly and violent behaviour spreads to primary schools, the second-biggest teachers' union said yesterday.

Many schools do not have firm policies to deal with indiscipline and fail to support teachers who have to endure a daily diet of insults as they struggle to keep control, according to the National Association of Schoolmasters Union of Women Teachers.

The union says it has noticed a surge in complaints over the past year which it attributes partly to the closure of special schools and the inclusion of children with behavioural problems in mainstream classes. Lack of respect for older people and authority means pupils are less easy to shame into contrition, say teachers.

The issue dominated the first day of debate at the union's annual conference in Brighton, where teachers stressed that a declining standard of behaviour was not confined to deprived parts of the inner cities.

Ralph Robins, the union's primary liaison officer in Cornwall, said teachers at 18 of the 20 primary schools he visited last term had problems with discipline. 'Cornwall is a delightful area but pupils still get rowdy and many of the staff tell me there is a surge towards questioning the authority of the class teacher,' he said.

Complaints about behaviour from primary school teachers were growing, said Mike Wilson, from Newark and Sherwood.

'Children as young as five and six are violent and disruptive. There are children who bite, scream and throw furniture and others who continually question staff, quoting their perceived human rights,' he said.

By Liz Lightfoot, Education Correspondent

'Why should I?' they say, and 'It's not fair.' Primary schools tended to be sympathetic to the children and did not want to exclude them because they were little. 'When they misbehave in this way then I say they are no longer little,' he said.

Diet contributed to poor behaviour, said Joy Higgins, from Essex. She had recently returned to classroom teaching and noticed a deterioration in behaviour. 'I see my form for registration three times a day. In the morning they are fine and human and you can hold a conversation with them.

Children of five are asserting their 'human right' to do as they please

'After break they are a bit rowdy and after lunch they are bouncing off the walls.'

Miss Higgins said she called it the 'sugar effect'. One pupil had been behaving so strangely that she asked if he was on drugs. He said he had just eaten three doughnuts. Research had shown that cutting out sugary cakes and drinks reduced asthma attacks and improved concentration and behaviour.

'We need to ban all recognised junk food being sold in vending machines and persuade parents not to put it in lunch boxes,' she said.

David Ward, from Sheffield, said poor behaviour was a common reason for teachers leaving the profession.

Applying continual, low-level discipline ground them down and prevented them from teaching. More serious incidents were also more common and he had received report recently of a teacher being stabbed in the arm with a compass and another hit on the head by a board rubber. The fire alarm had been activated by pupils 40 times in one day at one secondary school.

In one school, between 20 and 40 pupils were allowed to wander the corridors during class while at another pupils regularly spat on staff and each other from three floors up, said Mr Ward.

In Merseyside a case worker said he had dealt with three violent incidents in just over a week in one school. 'He told me that he had been a representative for the union for 30 years and had seen nothing like it,' said John Mayes, a national executive member.

'Often pupils start to become aggressive and disruptive in year seven, when they first move from primary schools where they have had one teacher for most of the day. They find they are chopping and changing and some cannot cope with the sheer numbers of children around them,' he said.

Many of the delegates blamed the Government's policy of inclusion, which meant pupils with severe behavioural problems being moved into mainstream classes as special schools closed. Just one child with behavioural problems could disrupt the education of the rest of the class, said Peter Tippets, from Hampshire.

'They see that if a disturbed pupil convincingly defies the authority of the teacher there is nothing that the teacher can do about it and the defiance spreads,' he said.

The union voted unanimously to call for a reversal of the policy of including violent and disruptive pupils in mainstream schools. It also urged automatic and permanent exclusion for violent and disruptive pupils.

30 March 2005

State-sanctioned violence?

Charities attack 'state-sanctioned violence' on children

The government has 'torn up' crucial parts of the UN treaty on children's rights by failing to protect vulnerable children, including young offenders and asylum seekers, a powerful coalition of charities warns today.

The Children's Rights Alliance for England (CRAE), representing more than 320 organisations, says the government is defying UN recommendations by sanctioning policies such as the use of physical restraint techniques, including a 'karate chop to the nose' on juveniles in custody.

The government's record over the past year in taking steps to abide by the UN Convention on the Rights of the Child is even worse than over the previous 12 months, according to a critical annual progress report by CRAE. Out of 78 areas where the UN called on the UK three years ago to change, significant progress has been made this year in only 16, compared with 17 in 2004, the alliance says.

Its report highlights in particular the use of so-called 'nose, rib and thumb distractions' – restraint techniques authorised by ministers for use in the four secure training centres (STCs) holding young people aged 12-17 in England and Wales.

Government figures obtained by CRAE under freedom of information

By Lucy Ward, social affairs correspondent

legislation show the techniques were used 768 times in STCs in the past 12 months, resulting in 51 injuries.

The three permitted distractions involve a blow to the nose – by far the most common restraint and employed 449 times – bending the thumb back (287 times) and grasping the ribs (32 times).

Ministers have said the restraints are used only rarely. But Carolyne Willow, CRAE's national coordinator, said: 'With a total of 768 uses, you are looking at four per unit per week. That is not rare, it's systematic. We see it as state-sanctioned violence on children.'

An inquiry into restraint, strip-searching and segregation in child custody, headed by Lord Carlile, is expected to report in the new year.

Meanwhile, CRAE has written to the European Committee for the Prevention of Torture to ask it to visit the four secure training centres to check the safety and wellbeing of children there.

CRAE's latest report also condemns the numbers of asylum-seeking children detained with their families – totalling 2,000 each year – and the lack of provision of formal education in detention centres.

Out of 78 areas where the UN called on the UK three years ago to change, significant progress has been made this year in only 16, compared with 17 in 2004

In its overview, CRAE welcomes government moves to transform children's services, under the Every Child Matters initiative, and the appointment of England's first children's commissioner.

But it claims the government has 'torn up the treaty for juvenile offenders and young asylum-seekers', and calls for an immediate review of children's law and policy in preparation for further scrutiny of the UK by the UN Committee on the Rights of the Child in 2009.
21 November 2005
© *Guardian Newspapers Limited 2005*

Child labour

Information from Anti-Slavery International

> 'Child labour has serious consequences that stay with the individual and with society for far longer than the years of childhood. Young workers not only face dangerous working conditions. They face long-term physical, intellectual and emotional stress. They face an adulthood of unemployment and illiteracy.'
> United Nations Secretary-General Kofi Annan

> 'We have no time for study and education, no time to play and rest, we are exposed to unsafe working conditions and we are not protected.'
> Children's Forum Against the Most Intolerable Forms of Child Labour, Bangkok, 1997

How big is the problem?

The International Labour Organization estimates there are 246 million working children aged between five and 17.

- 179 million are estimated to work in the worst forms of child labour – one in every eight of the world's five- to 17-years-olds
- 111 million children under 15 are in hazardous work and should be 'immediately withdrawn from this work'
- 8.4 million children are in slavery, trafficking, debt bondage and other forms of forced labour, forced recruitment for armed conflict, prostitution, pornography and other illicit activities
- Girls are particularly in demand for domestic work
- Around 70 per cent of child workers carry out unpaid work for their families.

Trafficking

Trafficking involves transporting people away from the communities in which they live, by the threat or use of violence, deception, or coercion so they can be exploited as forced or enslaved workers for sex or labour. When children are trafficked, no violence, deception or coercion needs to be involved, it is merely the act of transporting them into exploitative work which constitutes trafficking.

Increasingly, children are also bought and sold within and across national borders. They are trafficked for sexual exploitation, for begging, and for work on construction sites, plantations and into domestic work. The vulnerability of these children is even greater when they arrive in another country. Often they do not have contact with their families and are at the mercy of their employers.

today's fight for tomorrow's freedom

Why do children work?

- Most children work because their families are poor and their labour is necessary for their survival. Discrimination on grounds including gender, race or religion also plays its part in why some children work.

Some types of work make useful, positive contributions to a child's development. Work can help children learn about responsibility and develop particular skills that will benefit them and the rest of society. Often, work is a vital source of income that helps to sustain children and their families.

However, across the world, millions of children do extremely hazardous work in harmful conditions, putting their health, education, personal and social development, and even their lives at risk. These are some of the circumstances they face:

- Full-time work at a very early age
- Dangerous workplaces
- Excessive working hours
- Subjection to psychological, verbal, physical and sexual abuse
- Obliged to work by circumstances or individuals
- Limited or no pay
- Work and life on the streets in bad conditions
- Inability to escape from the poverty cycle – no access to education.

- Children are often employed and exploited because, compared to adults, they are more vulnerable, cheaper to hire and are less likely to demand higher wages or better working conditions. Some employers falsely argue that children are particularly suited to certain types of work because of their small size and 'nimble fingers'.
- For many children, school is not an option. Education can be expensive and some parents feel that what their children

will learn is irrelevant to the realities of their everyday lives and futures. In many cases, school is also physically inaccessible or lessons are not taught in the child's mother tongue, or both.

- As well as being a result of poverty, child labour also perpetuates poverty. Many working children do not have the opportunity to go to school and often grow up to be unskilled adults trapped in poorly paid jobs, and in turn will look to their own children to supplement the family's income.

As well as being a result of poverty, child labour also perpetuates poverty

---

Case studies

Sylvia* in Tanzania worked as a domestic. Despite only being a young teenager, she worked long hours cooking, cleaning and doing the majority of household chores. She was made to sleep on the floor, was only given leftovers to eat and was not paid for her labour. When one of the men in the household severely beat her for refusing his sexual advances, she fled. A neighbour referred her to the local organisation Kivulini which provided her with safe shelter and compensation from her 'employer'.

When Ahmed* was five years old he was trafficked from Bangladesh to the United Arab Emirates to be a camel jockey. He was forced to train and race camels in Dubai for three years.

'*I was scared … If I made a mistake I was beaten with a stick. When I said I wanted to go home I was told I never would. I didn't enjoy camel racing, I was really afraid. I fell off many times. When I won prizes several times, such as money and a car, the camel owner took everything. I never got anything, no money, nothing; my family also got nothing.*'

Ahmed was only returned home after a Bangladesh official identified him during a visit to Dubai in

Economic costs of child labour

Total economic costs and benefits of eliminating child labour over the period 2000-2020

	US$ billion, at purchasing power parity
Economic costs	
Education supply	493.3
Transfer implementation	10.7
Interventions	9.4
Opportunity costs	246.8
Total costs	**760.3**
Economic benefits	
Education	5,078.4
Health	28.0
Total benefits	**5,106.4**
Net economic benefits (total benefits - total costs)	4,346.1
Transfer payments	213.6
Net financial benefit (net economic benefit - transfer payments)	**4,132.5**

Source: International Labour Organization, Investing in Every Child: An economic study on the costs and benefits of eliminating child labour, International Programme on the Elimination of Child Labour, ILO, Geneva, 2004

November 2002. Our local partner Bangladesh National Women Lawyers' Association provided him with the specialist support and help he needed to resume his life with his family.
*Names changed

Child labour in the cocoa industry

Forced and child labour are present in the cocoa industry. Anti-Slavery International is working with governments in West Africa, Europe

Where do children work?

- On the land
- In households – as domestic workers
- In factories – making products such as matches, fireworks and glassware
- On the street – as beggars
- Outdoor industry: brick kilns, mines, construction
- In bars, restaurants and tourist establishments
- In sexual exploitation
- As soldiers.

Export industries account for only an estimated five per cent of child labour.

The majority of working children are in agriculture – an estimated 70 per cent. Child domestic work in the houses of others is thought to be the single largest employer of girls worldwide.

and the US, as well as with the cocoa industry, to stop this practice.

What do children want?

Children in several countries have formed their own organisations and movements to force leaders to hear their concerns and take action to improve a dire situation. Such movements include Niños y Adolescentes Trabajadores (NATS) in Latin America, the African Movement for Working Children and Youth in Africa and Bhima Sangha in South Asia.

The African Movement wants the realisation of 12 rights in particular, and they are:

- Right to vocational training
- Right to remain in our villages (not to have to go to the cities)
- Right to exercise our working activities in safety
- Right to light and limited work
- Right to rest during illness
- Right to be respected
- Right to be listened to
- Right to healthcare
- Right to learn to read and write
- Right to play and have free time
- Right to express and organise ourselves
- Right to equitable justice in case of problems.

At their fifth international conference in 2000, the Movement declared that:

'In those places where we are organised, our 12 rights have considerably progressed for us and for other working children and youth.

We can now learn to read and write, we benefit from better healthcare, we can express ourselves, we are respected by everyone as well as by the judicial system, we are well treated and can work in safer environments working in a manner compatible with our capacities and can sometimes rest. We are now able to have more leisure time and fewer children leave the villages after we went to tell them of the dangers.'

Children are often employed and exploited because, compared to adults, they are more vulnerable, cheaper to hire and are less likely to demand higher wages or better working conditions

---

Child soldiers

There are about 300,000 child soldiers involved in over 30 areas of conflict worldwide, some even younger than 10 years old. Child soldiers fight on the front line, and also work in support roles; girls are often obliged to be sex slaves or 'soldiers' wives'. Children involved in conflict are severely affected by their experiences and can suffer from long-term trauma. The Optional Protocol to the Convention on the Rights of the Child entered into force on 12 February 2002, which encourages governments to raise the age of voluntary recruitment into the armed forces and explicitly states that no person under the age of 18 should be sent into battle.

The United Kingdom, which has the lowest minimum recruitment age in Europe at 16, ratified the Optional Protocol on 24 June 2003. The Government, however, added a declaration to reserve the right to send under-18s into hostilities 'if there is a genuine military need' or 'due to the nature or urgency of the situation'. This clause is in direct conflict with the spirit of the Protocol, which urges that states

'take all feasible measures to ensure that members of their armed forces who have not attained the age of 18 years old do not take a direct part in hostilities'.

Action against child labour
International law

International law forms the basis of our work against the worst forms of child labour. The Conventions of the International Labour Organization, the 1926 and 1956 Slavery Conventions and the UN Convention on the Rights of the Child are the major tools we use.

- Article 32 of the UN Convention on the Rights of the Child (1989):

'State Parties recognise the right of the child to be protected from economic exploitation and from performing any work that is likely to be hazardous or to interfere with the child's education or to be harmful to the child's health or physical, mental, spiritual, moral or social development.'

- Convention 182 of the International Labour Organization (1999):

The main aim of Convention 182 is to eliminate the worst forms of child labour. It stresses that immediate action is needed to tackle the worst exploitation of children, and that measures taken by the authorities should start as soon as the government is able following ratification. The main provisions of the convention are to clarify which situations should be classified as the worst forms of child labour, and to specify what governments must do to prohibit and eliminate them. A copy of the full text of Convention 182 can be found on the ILO website.

- Reproduced with kind permission from Anti-Slavery International 2006. Join the fight for freedom 1807-2007 at: www.antislavery.org/2007.

© Anti-Slavery International 2006

Key statistics on child labour

Information from the International Labour Organization

- 246 million children are child labourers.
- 73 million working children are less than 10 years old.
- No country is immune: There are 2.5 million working children in the developed economies, and another 2.5 million in transition economies.
- Every year, 22,000 children die in work-related accidents.
- The largest number of working children – 127 million – age 14 and under are in the Asia-Pacific region.
- Sub-Saharan Africa has the largest proportion of working children: nearly one-third of children age 14 and under (48 million children).
- Most children work in the informal sector, without legal or regulatory protection:
- 70% in agriculture, commercial hunting and fishing or forestry;
- 8% in manufacturing;
- 8% in wholesale and retail trade, restaurants and hotels;
- 7% in community, social and personal service, such as domestic work.
- 8.4 million children are trapped in slavery, trafficking, debt bondage, prostitution, pornography and other illicit activities.
- 1.2 million of these children have been trafficked.

Source: International Labour Organization

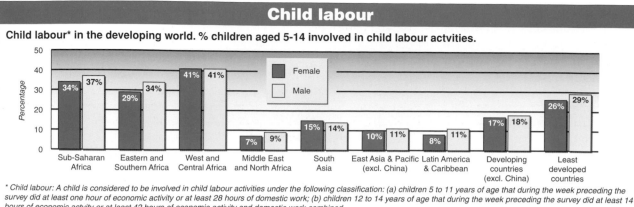

Child labour

Child labour* in the developing world. % children aged 5-14 involved in child labour actvities.

Legend: ■ Female □ Male

Region	Female	Male
Sub-Saharan Africa	34%	37%
Eastern and Southern Africa	29%	34%
West and Central Africa	41%	41%
Middle East and North Africa	7%	9%
South Asia	15%	14%
East Asia & Pacific (excl. China)	10%	11%
Latin America & Caribbean	8%	11%
Developing countries (excl. China)	17%	18%
Least developed countries	26%	29%

* Child labour: A child is considered to be involved in child labour activities under the following classification: (a) children 5 to 11 years of age that during the week preceding the survey did at least one hour of economic activity or at least 28 hours of domestic work; (b) children 12 to 14 years of age that during the week preceding the survey did at least 14 hours of economic actvity or at least 42 hours of economic activity and domestic work combined.

Source: Multiple Indicator Cluster Surveys (MICS) and Demographic and Health Surveys (DHS)

Forced commercial exploitation

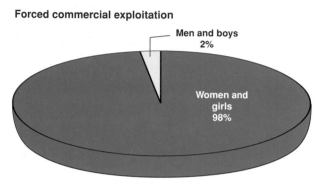

Men and boys 2%
Women and girls 98%

Source: Internation Labour Organization, A Global Alliance against Forced Labour, ILO, Geneva, 2005

Children in unconditional worst forms* of child labour and exploitation

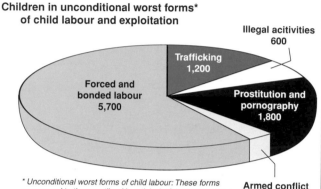

Illegal acitivities 600
Trafficking 1,200
Forced and bonded labour 5,700
Prostitution and pornography 1,800
Armed conflict 300

* Unconditional worst forms of child labour: These forms correspond to those outlined in article 3 of the International Labour Organization Convention No 182

Source: International Labour Organization, Every Child Counts: New global estimates on child labour, ILO, International Programme on the Elimination of Child Labour, Statistical Informational and Monitoring Programme on Child Labour, April 2002

Children and physical punishment

Speaking up – issues affecting Scotland's children

Children deserve the same protection from assault as adults. CHILDREN 1ST works to put an end to the physical punishment of children.

We firmly believe that adults should not be allowed to hit children. We also recognise that parents need to discipline their children. In order to protect the rights and interests of children, and equip parents with effective forms of discipline, CHILDREN 1ST works to establish a culture in which hitting children is never acceptable. This requires both public education on positive, non-violent forms of discipline, as well as legal reform to give children the same protection from assault as adults.

What is physical punishment?
Physical punishment is the use of physical force with the intention of causing a child to experience pain, but not injury, to correct or control the child's behaviour.

Background
Until 2003, a person with the lawful charge of a child under the age of 16 could administer physical punishment to that child under the Children and Young Persons (Scotland) Act 1937. The Children (Scotland) Act 1995 required that, in exercising this right, adults must act in 'the interests of the child'. While outlawing the assault, ill-treatment or neglect of a child, the 1937 Act therefore permitted the physical punishment of children so long as it amounted to 'reasonable chastisement'.

Over the years, physical punishment was banned in schools, publicly funded pre-school education, children's homes and foster care, until physical punishment could only take place within the family.

In 1998, however, the European Court of Human Rights found that the law in the UK regulating the physical punishment of children did not provide adequate protection. In *A v UK*, a nine-year-old boy who had been repeatedly beaten with a garden cane appealed to the Court under Article 3 of the European Convention on Human Rights which states that:

'No one shall be subjected to torture or to inhumane or degrading treatment.'

The Court held that beating with a garden cane with force on more than one occasion reached a level of severity prohibited by Article 3 and that the law in the UK failed to protect the boy. In reaching its decision as to whether or not the physical punishment constituted reasonable chastisement, the Court took into account the nature and context of the treatment, its duration, its physical and mental effects, and the sex, age and state of health of the child.

International law

The UK is a signatory to the United Nations Convention on the Rights of the Child. The Committee on the Rights of the Child periodically monitors our compliance with the Convention. In its most recent report, published in October 2002, the Committee reminded the UK that it had ignored its previous recommendations and those of the European Committee on Economic, Social and Cultural Rights to better protect children from physical punishment. The Committee 'deeply regretted' that the UK had persisted in retaining the defence of reasonable chastisement and had taken no significant action towards prohibiting all corporal punishment of children in the family. The Committee also stated that: 'governmental proposals to limit rather than to remove the "reasonable chastisement" defence do not comply with the principles and provisions of the Convention... particularly since they constitute a serious violation of the dignity of the child... Moreover, they suggest that some forms of corporal punishment are acceptable and therefore undermine educational measures to promote positive and non-violent discipline.'

The Committee went on to advise the UK to: 'promote positive, participatory and non-violent forms of discipline and respect for children's equal right to human dignity and physical integrity, engaging with children and parents and all those who work with and for them, and carry out public education programmes on the negative consequences of corporal punishment.'

The current legal position in Scotland

Despite the Committee's recommendations, in 2003, the Scottish Parliament passed the Criminal Justice (Scotland) Act. Section 51 of that Act prevents adults using implements, delivering blows to the head and shaking children as a physical punishment. While these specific practices are now prohibited, parents continue to enjoy special protection from the law when they physically punish a child.

Smacking is not an effective way to teach children discipline

---

In 'Children, physical punishment and the law: a guide for parents in Scotland', the Scottish Executive states that if a court is investigating the physical punishment of a child, as well as considering the actions prohibited by Section 51, it will consider:
- the child's age;
- what was done to the child, for what reason and what the circumstances were;
- the duration of the punishment and the frequency;
- how it affected the child (physically and mentally); and
- other issues personal to the child, such as their gender and state of health.

The Scottish Executive's guide also goes on to say that smacking is not an advisable method of disciplining children because it:
- can be dangerous. Adults, particularly if they are angry, can forget how delicate children are. What can feel like a light slap to an adult can potentially cause real harm to a small child;
- sets children the wrong example. Rather than correcting misbehaviour, smacking can teach children to hit out at people who are doing things they do not like, or who do not do what the child wants;

- has effects which last long after the physical pain dies away. Young children will not necessarily associate the physical punishment with their behaviour. It can make them angry and resentful, and can be damaging to their confidence and self-esteem; and
- smacking is not an effective way to teach children discipline.

Physical punishment in other countries

The physical punishment of children is illegal in 14 countries – Austria, Croatia, Cyprus, Denmark, Finland, Germany, Iceland, Israel, Italy, Latvia, Norway, Romania, Sweden and the Ukraine. In twelve of these countries, the ban on hitting children is a result of clear legislation outlawing the practice. In Italy and Israel, Supreme Court rulings have prohibited any form of physical punishment.

In many countries, legal reform has been accompanied by a high profile information campaign on positive parenting. In Germany, the introduction of the law was accompanied by a public education campaign entitled 'More respect for children'. One of its slogans was 'Help instead of punishment', stressing the fact that the law was intended to change public opinion and provide families with a means to move away from reliance on using force to resolve problems. The campaign was funded by central government, but was implemented by a combination of federal and local authorities, as well as non-governmental organisations.

Why ban physical punishment?

CHILDREN 1ST has welcomed the Scottish Parliament's attempts to ban some forms of punishment, but continues to campaign for full legal reform. A ban on all forms of physical punishment is needed to:
- support parents and carers, by providing a clear legal basis for the promotion of positive, non-violent forms of discipline by statutory and voluntary bodies working with families. Such discipline would reduce stress, improve family relationships and

create sociable, selfdisciplined and well-motivated children;

■ tackle violence. Research shows that children firmly believe that physical punishment is wrong and that it sets a bad example to young children by teaching them that the use of violence is an acceptable way to respond;

■ enhance child protection measures. A ban would enable child protection workers to give parents of children at risk of abuse a clear message that no level of physical punishment is acceptable. It would also ensure that children have a consistent level of protection which does not vary according to who is looking after them; and

■ assert the equal human right of children to protection of their physical integrity. Challenging routine violence to children, the weakest members of society, is as important as challenging routine violence to women.

Physical punishment and domestic violence

CHILDREN 1ST has welcomed the public investment in measures to reduce domestic violence and we are particularly pleased at the Scottish Executive's plans to help children who witness domestic violence. However, we remain concerned that so little attention has been focused on the needs of children who are hit by their parents. CHILDREN 1ST believes that protecting children requires zero tolerance on violence, both in the community and in the home.

Positive parenting

Being a parent is perhaps the most valuable, responsible and demanding job that you can do. There is no one correct way of bringing up children and it is rarely 'plain sailing'. Some parents and carers need help to cope and that can include picking up a leaflet, accessing support from families, friends and organisations, or calling a helpline. It is exceptional if adults manage to bring up a child without any help or support! With this in mind, in 1999, CHILDREN 1ST set up ParentLine Scotland, the national telephone helpline. Twenty-nine per cent of calls to the helpline from parents and carers relate to behaviour and discipline issues.

It is the experience of CHILDREN 1ST that many parents are already upset that they physically punish their child, but that they do not know what else to do. An analysis of calls concerning physical punishment to ParentLine Scotland shows that adults say one of two things:

'I've just smacked my child – I know it doesn't work, but what else can I do?' 'I don't want to smack my children, but I don't know what else to do.'

Parents do not like hitting their children and welcome effective, non-violent alternatives. A father who attended a family support project run by CHILDREN 1ST said:

'I learnt different ways to cope with the kids' behaviour. I've found ways to keep them occupied. I've learnt how to discipline your children without using force.'

CHILDREN 1ST understands that many parents want to get help so that they can learn to stop hitting their children. We believe that parents should be able to access information and services which meet their needs. We have urged the Scottish Executive to actively promote positive parenting and alternative forms of discipline.

Myths about a ban on hitting children

The campaign to ban the hitting of children raises a number of anxieties and questions.

Will a ban lead to parents being prosecuted for trivial smacks?
No. Just as adults are not prosecuted for trivial assaults on other adults, parents will not be prosecuted for trivial smacks. Instead, a ban on smacking coupled with a public education campaign is likely to reduce the need for prosecutions through changes in parental attitudes and practice. This is what happened in Sweden, where there has been no increase in prosecutions for parental assaults of children since the ban was introduced.

Will a ban lead to more children being taken into care?
No. A ban will not lead to more compulsory social work intervention in families or to the removal of children into care. Again, the Swedish experience shows a marked decline in out-of-family placements of children and of compulsory forms of intervention since the ban began.

Will a ban prevent parents using physical measures to restrain their children?
No. A ban will not prevent parents from using physical measures to protect or restrain their children. Nor will a ban absolve them of their duty to teach children good manners, the difference between right and wrong, and how to behave respectfully towards others. Indeed, we can expect the greater use of positive, consistent and effective forms of discipline as a consequence of a ban on hitting children.

If parents are not going to be prosecuted, is a ban pointless?
A ban will result in significant changes in attitudes and practice. A ban will not represent an unenforceable or pointless measure. In Sweden, the majority of the public supported smacking before the ban, but now only 6% of under 35-year-olds support even the mildest form of physical punishment.

■ The above information is reprinted with kind permission from. CHILDREN 1ST, the working name of the Royal Scottish Society for Prevention of Cruelty to Children. Visit www.children1st.org.uk for more information.

© Children 1st

The Universal Declaration of Human Rights

Articles of the Universal Declaration of Human Rights, from the website of the Office of the High Commissioner for Human Rights

Article 1

All human beings are born free and equal in dignity and rights. They are endowed with reason and conscience and should act towards one another in a spirit of brotherhood.

Article 2

Everyone is entitled to all the rights and freedoms set forth in this Declaration, without distinction of any kind, such as race, colour, sex, language, religion, political or other opinion, national or social origin, property, birth or other status.

> *No one shall be held in slavery or servitude; slavery and the slave trade shall be prohibited in all their forms*

Furthermore, no distinction shall be made on the basis of the political, jurisdictional or international status of the country or territory to which a person belongs, whether it be independent, trust, non-self-governing or under any other limitation of sovereignty.

Article 3

Everyone has the right to life, liberty and security of person.

Article 4

No one shall be held in slavery or servitude; slavery and the slave trade shall be prohibited in all their forms.

Article 5

No one shall be subjected to torture or to cruel, inhuman or degrading treatment or punishment.

Article 6

Everyone has the right to recognition everywhere as a person before the law.

Article 7

All are equal before the law and are entitled without any discrimination to equal protection of the law. All are entitled to equal protection against any discrimination in violation of this Declaration and against any incitement to such discrimination.

Article 8

Everyone has the right to an effective remedy by the competent national tribunals for acts violating the fundamental rights granted him by the constitution or by law.

Article 9

No one shall be subjected to arbitrary arrest, detention or exile.

Article 10

Everyone is entitled in full equality to a fair and public hearing by an independent and impartial tribunal, in the determination of his rights and obligations and of any criminal charge against him.

Article 11

1. Everyone charged with a penal offence has the right to be presumed innocent until proved guilty according to law in a public trial at which he has had all the guarantees necessary for his defence.

2. No one shall be held guilty of any penal offence on account of any act or omission which did not constitute a penal offence, under national or international law, at the time when it was committed. Nor shall a heavier penalty be imposed than the one that was applicable at the time the penal offence was committed.

Article 12

No one shall be subjected to arbitrary interference with his privacy, family, home or correspondence, nor to attacks upon his honour and reputation. Everyone has the right to the protection of the law against such interference or attacks.

Article 13

1. Everyone has the right to freedom of movement and residence within the borders of each State.

2. Everyone has the right to leave any country, including his own, and to return to his country.

Article 14

1. Everyone has the right to seek and to enjoy in other countries asylum from persecution.
2. This right may not be invoked in the case of prosecutions genuinely arising from non-political crimes or from acts contrary to the purposes and principles of the United Nations.

Article 15

1. Everyone has the right to a nationality.
2. No one shall be arbitrarily deprived of his nationality nor denied the right to change his nationality.

> *Everyone has the right to take part in the government of his country, directly or through freely chosen representatives*

Article 16

1. Men and women of full age, without any limitation due to race, nationality or religion, have the right to marry and to found a family. They are entitled to equal rights as to marriage, during marriage and at its dissolution.
2. Marriage shall be entered into only with the free and full consent of the intending spouses.
3. The family is the natural and fundamental group unit of society and is entitled to protection by society and the State.

Article 17

1. Everyone has the right to own property alone as well as in association with others.
2. No one shall be arbitrarily deprived of his property.

Article 18

Everyone has the right to freedom of thought, conscience and religion; this right includes freedom to change his religion or belief, and freedom, either alone or in community with others and in public or private, to manifest his religion or belief in teaching, practice, worship and observance.

Article 19

Everyone has the right to freedom of opinion and expression; this right includes freedom to hold opinions without interference and to seek, receive and impart information and ideas through any media and regardless of frontiers.

Article 20

1. Everyone has the right to freedom of peaceful assembly and association.
2. No one may be compelled to belong to an association.

Article 21

1. Everyone has the right to take part in the government of his country, directly or through freely chosen representatives.
2. Everyone has the right to equal access to public service in his country.
3. The will of the people shall be the basis of the authority of government; this will shall be expressed in periodic and genuine elections which shall be by universal and equal suffrage and shall be held by secret vote or by equivalent free voting procedures.

Article 22

Everyone, as a member of society, has the right to social security and is entitled to realization, through national effort and international co-operation and in accordance with the organisation and resources of each State, of the economic, social and cultural rights indispensable for his dignity and the free development of his personality.

Article 23

1. Everyone has the right to work, to free choice of employment, to just and favourable conditions of work and to protection against unemployment.
2. Everyone, without any discrimination, has the right to equal pay for equal work.
3. Everyone who works has the right to just and favourable remuneration ensuring for himself and his family an existence worthy of human dignity, and supplemented, if necessary, by other means of social protection.
4. Everyone has the right to form and to join trade unions for the protection of his interests.

Article 24

Everyone has the right to rest and leisure, including reasonable limitation of working hours and periodic holidays with pay.

Article 25

1. Everyone has the right to a standard of living adequate for the health and well-being of himself and of his family, including food, clothing, housing and medical care and necessary social services, and the right to security in the event of unemployment, sickness, disability, widowhood, old age or other lack of livelihood in circumstances beyond his control.
2. Motherhood and childhood are entitled to special care and assistance. All children, whether born in or out of wedlock, shall enjoy the same social protection.

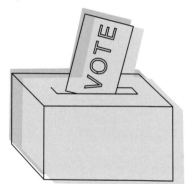

Article 26

1. Everyone has the right to education. Education shall be free, at least in the elementary and fundamental stages. Elementary education shall be compulsory. Technical and professional education shall be made generally available and higher education shall be equally accessible to all on the basis of merit.
2. Education shall be directed to the full development of the human personality and to the strengthening of respect for human rights and fundamental freedoms. It shall promote understanding, tolerance and friendship among all nations, racial or religious groups, and shall further the activities of the United Nations for the maintenance of peace.
3. Parents have a prior right to choose the kind of education that shall be given to their children.

Article 27

1. Everyone has the right freely to participate in the cultural life of the community, to enjoy the arts and to share in scientific advancement and its benefits.
2. Everyone has the right to the protection of the moral and material interests resulting from any scientific, literary or artistic production of which he is the author.

Article 28

Everyone is entitled to a social and international order in which the rights and freedoms set forth in this Declaration can be fully realised.

Article 29

1. Everyone has duties to the community in which alone the free and full development of his personality is possible.
2. In the exercise of his rights and freedoms, everyone shall be subject only to such limitations as are determined by law solely for the purpose of securing due recognition and respect for the rights and freedoms of others and of meeting the just requirements of morality, public order and the general welfare in a democratic society.
3. These rights and freedoms may in no case be exercised contrary to the purposes and principles of the United Nations.

Article 30

Nothing in this Declaration may be interpreted as implying for any State, group or person any right to engage in any activity or to perform any act aimed at the destruction of any of the rights and freedoms set forth herein.

■ The above information is reprinted with kind permission from the Office of the High Commissioner for Human Rights.

© OHCHR

Human Rights Act

Frequently asked questions

General information on the Human Rights Act 1998

What is the Human Rights Act?
The United Kingdom signed and ratified the European Convention on Human Rights (ECHR). This Convention is a binding international agreement that the UK helped to draft and has sought to comply with for over half a century. The Convention enshrines fundamental civil and political rights, but for many years it was not part of our own law. Using the Convention usually meant taking a case to the European Court of Human Rights in Strasbourg. This was often time-consuming and expensive.

Since coming into force on 2 October 2000, the Human Rights Act has made rights from the ECHR (the Convention rights) enforceable in our own courts. This is much quicker and simpler than the old arrangement.

What does the Human Rights Act do?
The new law does three simple things about the rights and freedoms in the European Convention on Human Rights:

The Human Rights Act means that we can all be clearer about basic values and standards we share. That's a good idea when it comes to sorting out problems

i. It makes it unlawful for a public authority to violate Convention rights, unless, because of an Act of Parliament, it had no choice.
ii. It says that all UK legislation should be given a meaning that fits with the rights, if that's possible. If a Court says it's not possible, it will be up to Parliament to decide what to do.
iii. Cases can be dealt with in a UK Court or tribunal. You don't have to go to the European Court of Human Rights in Strasbourg.

This means that the Act makes it simpler for UK judges to help you if your rights are trampled on – and all your public services must do everything they can to prevent that happening in the first place.

More Eurolaw?
No. The Human Rights Act is British legislation. The European Convention on Human Rights, which is the source of the Act, was largely drafted by British lawyers and is a treaty agreement from the Council of Europe, not the European Union. The European Union has recently drawn up a Charter of Fundamental Rights, which is a separate matter.

What difference does the Human Rights Act make?
The Human Rights Act means that we can all be clearer about basic values and standards we share. That's a good idea when it comes to sorting out problems.

The Act means that all public authorities must pay proper attention to your rights when they are making decisions that affect you.

What is a public authority?
There is no express definition of 'public authority' in the Act but the term includes:

■ Government departments
■ Local authorities
■ Police, prison, immigration officers
■ Public prosecutors

- Courts and tribunals
- Non-departmental public bodies (NDPBs)
- Any person exercising a 'public function'.

Isn't this just a chancer's charter?
No. The Human Rights Act is about basic fairness for all people. It is about understanding the respect due to each of us. It is about recognising that some rights and freedoms are so important and so fundamental that they should be protected by law. It is not about getting people off on technicalities and our Courts have not treated it in that way.

> *The Human Rights Act is about basic fairness for all people. It is about recognising that some rights and freedoms are so important and so fundamental that they should be protected by law*

Doesn't the Human Rights Act mean that judges have more power than our elected politicians?
The Human Rights Act was carefully drafted to preserve the primacy of Parliament. Put simply, judges can't overrule Parliament. If a judge finds that a piece of primary legislation is incompatible with the Act, (s)he can make a 'declaration of incompatibility', but it remains for Parliament to decide what, if any, action to take.

Have the Courts been swamped by dubious claims made under the Human Rights Act?
No. Statistics from the first year of the Act being fully in force show only very small increases in the total work of the Courts. Senior judges themselves have commented that the Act has not disrupted the system, rather it has complemented it.

Is the Government setting up a Human Rights Commission?
The Government announced its intention to set up a Commission for Equality and Human Rights on 30 October 2003.

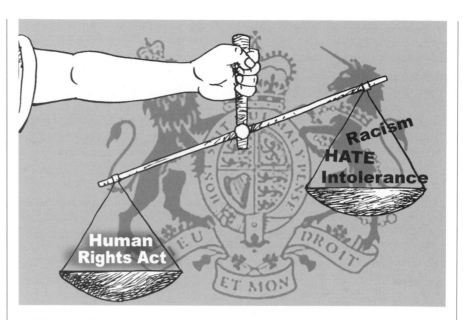

Help with a personal case
Where can I find help with a personal case?
If you believe that your Convention rights have been breached you should consider seeking legal advice. If you need help the Community Legal Service Direct brings together organisations offering legal and advice services throughout England and Wales. This Service also runs an information line on 0845 608 1122.

Is there any more detailed official guidance on bringing a case / my rights?
Yes, the Department for Constitutional Affairs has worked with the Bar Council to produce a Study Guide on the Human Rights Act.

How can I use the Act to enforce my human rights?
If you think that a public authority has breached your Convention rights, you can:
a. take the authority to court for breaching your rights
b. rely on the Convention rights in the course of any other proceedings involving a public authority, e.g. judicial review, criminal trial.

If you take the direct route as in (a), you generally have to bring proceedings within a year of the breach. The court can allow you to bring proceedings after a longer period if it thinks this is fair in all the circumstances. This is not necessarily straightforward and you should consider seeking advice from a solicitor or local advice bureau.

Who can bring a case under the Human Rights Act?
Proceedings under the Human Rights Act can only be brought by 'victims' of a breach of one or more Convention rights by a public authority. Interest groups and charities cannot bring actions unless they meet the 'victim test'. But they can assist those who do bring actions.

Will I still be able to take a case to Strasbourg?
Yes. But the European Court of Human Rights will want to know that you have exhausted all domestic remedies. This means that you must have taken your case to all the appropriate Courts / tribunals in this country before applying to Strasbourg. You should consider seeking advice from a solicitor or local advice bureau. The Community Legal Service can help put you in contact with advice providers in your local area.

Further information on the European Convention on Human Rights and other International Instruments
What ECHR Protocols has the UK signed up to?
The UK has ratified Protocols 1, 6 and 13. The UK has not yet ratified the other protocols containing substantive rights (Protocols 4, 7 and 12). These are under review.

How do Protocol rights get into the Human Rights Act?
The rights in Protocols 1 and 6 are already there. Those in other Protocols can be added in future

by order without the need for fresh primary legislation.

Will the UK introduce a right of individual petition under the United Nations treaties?

The Government has undertaken a review of the UK's obligations under various international treaties including the UN treaties. The outcome of this review will be announced later this year.

The European Union Charter of Fundamental Rights

What is the European Union Charter of Fundamental Rights?

The European Union Charter of Fundamental Rights sets out in a single text civil, political, economic and social rights enjoyed in the Member States.

These rights are grouped into six chapters:

- Dignity
- Freedoms
- Equality
- Solidarity
- Citizens' rights
- Justice.

The Charter is not intended to lay down new rights – but it draws existing rights together and makes them much more visible to the citizen. It was also intended to remind the Union institutions of the rights they should respect in discharging their responsibilities.

What is the Charter's legal status?

The Presidents of the European Parliament, the Council and the Commission signed and proclaimed the Charter on behalf of their institutions on 7 December 2000 in Nice. The Charter is a political declaration – it has no legal force. As such the future legal status of the Charter is a matter of current debate and will be decided by the Member States in the near future.

What's different from the European Convention on Human Rights?

Most national Governments have a list of citizens' basic rights and liberties which the State must respect. At European level we have the European Convention on Human Rights, but that system does not control the European Union's institutions. And the ECHR does not cover quite a lot of the fundamental rights and freedoms already agreed for the EU. So the Charter will make more visible to EU citizens that they have, for example, rights to vote in elections for the European Parliament, rights to work and set up businesses in other Member States, rights of access to EU documents and rights to complain to the EU ombudsman.

Will the Charter take power away from the UK Parliament?

Charter Article 51 states: 'This Charter does not extend the scope of application of Union law beyond the powers of the Union or establish any new power or task for the Union, or modify powers and tasks defined in the other Parts of the Constitution.' So the Charter will not extend Union powers as set out elsewhere in the EU Constitution treaty, and the Charter applies to the Member States only when they are implementing Union law. It is firmly established that the Charter shall not give any new powers to Europe.

'Social Europe' rights? Bad for business?

Many of the provisions in the so-called 'Solidarity' chapter of the Charter are guiding principles, not legal rights as such. The changes the UK helped to negotiate to the Charter's special rules of interpretation (especially Charter Article 52(5)) help clarify this. In any case the Charter does not allow the Union to go beyond the powers already agreed for it – and the UK helped negotiate changes to the Charter to make that crystal clear too.

Aren't most of the Charter rights outside EU competence?

The rights set out in the Charter do not in themselves give the EU any power to legislate – any such power must be set out in other parts of the EU Constitution Treaty. But EU action in other areas where it does have power to act under the Constitution Treaty may affect fundamental rights indirectly. In such cases a Charter right may be relevant even if it is outside EU competence as such.

Won't everyone be suing in Luxembourg under the Charter?

The Charter does not change the existing system of legal remedies at EU level. Member States and their courts remain the prime guardians of their peoples' rights.

Will the Charter will rewrite our system of criminal justice?

Nothing in the Charter changes the Union's powers as agreed by the Member States. The Charter's provisions about criminal justice are modelled closely on the ECHR, which is already basic law in the UK.

- The above information is re-printed with kind permission from the Department for Constitutional Affairs. For more information, please visit their website at www.dca.gov.uk.

© Crown copyright

DIGNITY | **FREEDOM** | **EQUALITY** | **SOLIDARITY** | **CITIZENS' RIGHTS** | **JUSTICE**

ILO releases major new study on forced labour

Says more than 12 million are trapped in forced labour worldwide

At least 12.3 million people are trapped in forced labour around the world, the International Labour Office (ILO) said in a new study released today. ILO Director-General Juan Somavia called forced labour 'a social evil which has no place in the modern world'.

The new report, entitled 'A global alliance against forced labour', says that nearly 10 million people are exploited through forced labour in the private economy, rather than imposed directly by states. Of these, the study estimates a minimum of 2.4 million to be victims of human trafficking.

Approximately one-fifth of all forced labourers globally are trafficked

---

The report also provides the first global estimate of the profits generated by the exploitation of trafficked women, children and men – US$ 32 billion each year, or an average of US$ 13,000 from every single trafficked forced labourer.

'Forced labour represents the underside of globalisation and denies people their basic rights and dignity,' Mr Somavia said. 'To achieve a fair globalisation and decent work for all, it is imperative to eradicate forced labour.'

The report is the most comprehensive analysis ever undertaken by an intergovernmental organisation of the facts and underlying causes of contemporary forced labour. It was prepared under the Follow Up to the Declaration on Fundamental Principles and Rights at Work adopted by the ILO in 1998 and will be discussed at the Organization's annual International Labour Conference in June.

The new study confirms that forced labour is a major global problem which is present in all regions and in all types of economy. Of the overall total, some 9.5 million forced labourers are in Asia, which is the region with the highest number; 1.3 million in Latin America and the Caribbean; 660,000 in sub-Saharan Africa; 260,000 in the Middle East and North Africa; 360,000 in industrialised countries; and 210,000 in transition countries.

Forced economic exploitation in such sectors as agriculture, construction, brick-making and informal sweatshop manufacturing is more or less evenly divided between the sexes. However, forced commercial sexual exploitation entraps almost entirely women and girls. In addition, children aged less than 18 years bear a heavy burden, comprising 40 to 50 per cent of all forced labour victims.

Approximately one-fifth of all forced labourers globally are traf-

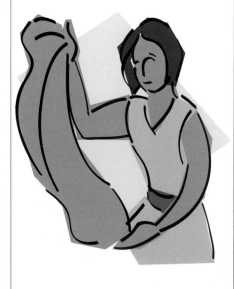

ficked but the proportion varies widely from region to region, the report says. In Asia, Latin America and sub-Saharan Africa, the proportion of trafficked persons is less than 20 per cent of all forced labour, while in industrialised and transition countries and in the Middle East and North Africa, trafficking accounts for more than 75 per cent of the total.

Most forced labour today is still exacted in developing countries where older forms of forced labour are sometimes transmuting into newer ones, notably in a range of informal sector activities, the report says. Debt bondage frequently affects minorities – including indigenous peoples – that have long experienced discrimination on the labour market, and locks them in a vicious cycle of poverty from which they find it ever more difficult to escape. Many victims are working in remote geographical areas, where labour inspection presents a particular challenge.

The report sheds new light on the emerging forms of forced labour affecting migrant workers, in particular irregular migrants in rich and poor destination countries alike. It also examines the labour market conditions under which forced labour is most likely to occur, such as where there are inadequate controls over recruitment agencies and subcontracting systems, or weak labour inspection.

The appearance of new forms of coercion in today's globalised economy also raises some difficult policy questions. The report examines the strong pressures to deregulate labour markets as part of the overall drive to reduce labour costs and thereby increase competitiveness.

'Forced labour is the very antithesis of decent work, the goal of the ILO,' says Mr Somavia.

'There is critical need for devising effective strategies against forced labour today. This requires a blend of law enforcement and ways of tackling the structural roots of forced labour, whether outmoded agrarian systems or poorly functioning labour markets.'

The report makes the case that forced labour can be abolished, but only if governments and national institutions pursue active polices, vigorous enforcement and show strong commitment to eradicating such treatment of human beings. It also presents the positive experience in selected countries that, with ILO assistance, are now tackling forced labour by adopting strong legislation and enforcement mechanisms, implementing policies and programmes to tackle the underlying causes, and helping victims rebuild their lives.

'Although the numbers are large, they are not so large as to make abolishing forced labour impossible,' Mr Somavia says. 'Thus, the ILO calls for a global alliance against forced labour involving governments, employers' and workers' organisations, development agencies and international financial institutions concerned with poverty reduction, and civil society including research and academic institutions. With political will and global commitment over the next decade, we believe forced labour can be relegated to history.'
11 May 2005

■ The above information is reprinted with kind permission from the International Labour Organization. Visit www.ilo.org for more information.
© International Labour Organization

What is modern slavery?

Information from Anti-Slavery International

For many people, the image that comes to mind when they hear the word slavery is the slavery of the Transatlantic Slave Trade. We think of the buying and selling of people, their shipment from one continent to another and the abolition of the trade in the early 1800s. Even if we know nothing about the slave trade, it is something we think of as part of our history rather than our present. But the reality is slavery continues TODAY.

Millions of men, women and children around the world are forced to lead lives as slaves. Although this exploitation is often not called slavery, the conditions are the same. People are sold like objects, forced to work for little or no pay and are at the mercy of their 'employers'.

Slavery exists today despite the fact that it is banned in most of the countries where it is practised. It is also prohibited by the 1948 Universal Declaration of Human Rights and the 1956 UN Supplementary Convention on the Abolition of Slavery, the Slave Trade and Institutions and Practices Similar to Slavery. Women from eastern Europe are bonded into prostitution, children are trafficked between West African countries and men are forced to work as slaves on Brazilian agricultural estates. Contemporary

slavery takes various forms and affects people of all ages, sex and race.

What is slavery?
Common characteristics distinguish slavery from other human rights violations. A slave is:
■ forced to work – through mental or physical threat;
■ owned or controlled by an 'employer', usually through mental or physical abuse or threatened abuse;
■ dehumanised, treated as a commodity or bought and sold as 'property';
■ physically constrained or has restrictions placed on his/her freedom of movement.

What types of slavery exist today?
Bonded labour affects at least 20 million* people around the world. People become bonded labourers by taking or being tricked into taking a loan for as little as the cost of medicine for a sick child. To repay the debt, many are forced to work long hours, seven days a week, up to 365 days a year. They receive basic food and shelter as 'payment' for their work, but may never pay off the loan, which can be passed down for generations.

Early and forced marriage affects women and girls who are married without choice and are forced into lives of servitude often accompanied by physical violence.

Forced labour affects people who are illegally recruited by individuals, governments or political parties and forced to work – usually under threat of violence or other penalties.

Slavery by descent is where people are either born into a slave class or are from a 'group' that society views as suited to being used as slave labour.

Trafficking involves the transport and/or trade of people – women, children and men – from one area to another for the purpose of forcing them into slavery conditions.

Worst forms of child labour affect an estimated 179 million** children around the world in work that is harmful to their health and welfare.
*UN
** ILO

■ Reproduced with kind permission from Anti-Slavery International 2006. Join the fight for freedom 1807-2007 at: www.antislavery.org/2007.
© Anti-Slavery International 2006

Modern forms of slavery in industrialised countries

Information from the International Labour Organization

A new report by the ILO estimates that more than 12 million people worldwide are victims of forced labour. But this modern-day form of slavery is not restricted to developing countries, and can also be found in industrialised countries, where approximately 360,000 people are forced to work. Two examples of this practice are migrant workers in the German meat industry, and fruit pickers in Florida, United States.

IMMOKALEE, Florida, United States – It is 4.30 in the morning. Night still hangs over the tiny town of Immokalee, Florida, but the road is lined with men in mangled work boots walking half-asleep towards a parking lot full of buses. They will take them, along dusty roads, to a tomato farm.

Inside a dark trailer, a man pulls on his boots and gets ready for work. 'My name is Luis. I am from Guatemala. Every morning at 4.30 I go to pick fruit. The work is very hard and pays very little', he says.

Luis shares a small trailer with 13 other men so he can save enough money to send to his family in Guatemala. The men sleep four to a bed but consider themselves lucky because they have basic electricity and plumbing.

But some of their fellow workers do not feel as lucky when it comes to working in the fields. 'There were guards in the fields with guns. The workers were being watched all the time and they were beaten if they tried to leave,' says Lucas Benitez from the Coalition of Immokalee Workers.

Lucas Benitez helped organize the Coalition of Immokalee Workers when he realised many of his co-workers were being held as bonded labourers. Lured by salaries that far outstrip what they could ever make in their home countries, workers like Luis can be trapped by debts owed to their contractors.

'Every year, hundreds of thousands of workers are trafficked into this country to work as forced labourers. If those numbers aren't shocking, I don't know what is,' comments Carlos Castillo from the Department of Justice in Miami, Florida.

In the last three years, the US Department of Justice has been able to prosecute increasing numbers of cases under the Trafficking Victims Protection Act, and develop regional anti-trafficking task forces in states like Florida. But according to the latest ILO global report on forced labour, the complex chains of contracting and subcontracting can affect major retail companies who do not realise the conditions under which their produce is being supplied.

After two years of negotiation, Yum Brands, the largest restaurant company in the world – owner of Taco Bell, Pizza Hut and other fast food chains – agreed to join with the Coalition of Immokalee Workers to improve wages and conditions of workers. The agreement with Taco Bell, whereby they pay one penny more, is very important, but it is the code of conduct the union and the company agreed on that will help end cases of abuse.

Migrant workers in the German meat industry

Workers in Romanian abattoirs have the same skills as their German colleagues but work for a fraction of their wages. With the opening up of Eastern Europe, they have been travelling to Germany in thousands. In Oldenburg, the centre of the German meat industry, unscrupulous middlemen bring migrant workers to big slaughterhouses. Some work for just 3 Euros an hour – a German worker would expect four times that amount.

As the Romanians went on strike when they did not receive the wages they had been promised, their employer sent men around to beat them up. 'They hit the door, they threw me down, they kicked me. I was sitting on the chair, they hit me. Look, this tooth, one is missing, and the other one is wobbly', says Daniel Kincza, one of the victims.

Wilfried Ideke, the owner of the slaughterhouse, was sentenced to three years' imprisonment for trafficking and employing workers illegally. The Romanian workers' case came to light because they took it to a union and went to court. According to the unions, this was not an isolated incident.

'It is modern-day slavery we're talking about: traffickers, middlemen who send employees here to Germany who are not fully informed about their job. Often there is no possibility of finding out more because they don't know the language. When they are drawing up the contract, they are lying to the workers,' explains Markus Dieterich from the German food industry union NGG.

Most Romanians have now left the German meat industry, as a bilateral agreement between Romania and Germany has come to an end. Today, the cars outside the meat processing factory – which has been taken over by a Danish company – are mostly Polish. An anonymous poster on a tree calls on butchers to protest against cheap foreign labour taking German jobs…

'Consumers want to buy meat and tomatoes at ever-lower prices. Most of them are unaware their meat has been prepared by migrant workers facing exploitation far from home,' says Roger Plant, main author of the report. 'A global alliance against forced labour must now be forged to ensure that this gross violation of the rights of women and men across the world is finally relegated to history.' *11 May 2005*

■ The above information is reprinted with kind permission from the International Labour Organization. For more information please visit their website at www.ilo.org.

© International Labour Organization

Refugees

Information from Human Rights Watch

Who

A refugee is someone with a well-founded fear of persecution on the basis of his or her race, religion, nationality, membership in a particular social group or political opinion, who is outside of his or her country of nationality and unable or unwilling to return. Refugees are forced from their countries by war, civil conflict, political strife or gross human rights abuses. There were an estimated 14.9 million refugees in the world in 2001 – people who had crossed an international border to seek safety – and at least 22 million internally displaced persons (IDPs) who had been uprooted within their own countries.

What

Enshrined in Article 14 of the 1948 Universal Declaration of Human Rights is the right 'to seek and to enjoy in other countries asylum from persecution'. This principle recognises that victims of human rights abuse must be able to leave their country freely and to seek refuge elsewhere. Governments frequently see refugees as a threat or a burden, refusing to respect this core principle of human rights and refugee protection.

Where

The global refugee crisis affects every continent and almost every country. In 2001, 78 per cent of all refugees came from 10 areas: Afghanistan, Angola, Burma, Burundi, Congo-Kinshasa, Eritrea, Iraq, the Palestinian territories, Somalia and Sudan. Palestinians are the world's oldest and largest refugee population, and make up more than one-fourth of all refugees. Asia hosts 45 per cent of all refugees, followed by Africa (30 per cent), Europe (19 per cent) and North America (5 per cent).

A refugee is someone with a well-founded fear of persecution

When

Throughout history, people have fled their homes to escape persecution. In the aftermath of World War II, the international community included the right to asylum in the 1948 Universal Declaration of Human Rights. In 1950, the Office of the United Nations High Commissioner for Refugees (UNHCR) was created to protect and assist refugees, and, in 1951, the United Nations adopted the Convention Relating to the Status of Refugees, a legally binding treaty that, by February 2002, had been ratified by 140 countries.

Why

In the past 50 years, states have largely regressed in their commitment to protect refugees, with the wealthy industrialised states of Europe, North America and Australia – which first established the international refugee protection system – adopting particularly hostile and restrictive policies. Governments have subjected refugees to arbitrary arrest, detention, denial of social and economic rights and closed borders. In the worst cases, the most fundamental principle of refugee protection, nonrefoulement, is violated, and refugees are forcibly returned to countries where they face persecution. Since September 11, many countries have pushed through emergency anti-terrorism legislation that curtails the rights of refugees.

How

Human Rights Watch believes the right to asylum is a matter of life and death and cannot be compromised. In our work to stop human rights abuses in countries around the world, we seek to address the root causes that force people to flee. We also advocate for greater protection for refugees and IDPs and for an end to the abuses they suffer when they reach supposed safety. Human Rights Watch calls on the United Nations and on governments everywhere to uphold their obligations to protect refugees and to respect their rights – regardless of where they are from or where they seek refuge.

■ Information from Human Rights Watch. Visit www.hrw.org for more.
© HRW

Big Brother at work

Ever wondered what it would have been like to share the Big Brother house with reality TV's new batch of hopefuls? Well, you may be closer than you think

By Work Rights Expert, Rachel Lewis

Hi-tech gadgetry and sophisticated surveillance techniques in the workplace make all of us vulnerable. Sure, most of us would agree that some things are totally unacceptable – if your colleague gets sacked for downloading and mailing hardcore porn or racist material, you're unlikely to feel too much sympathy. But in the majority of cases, it's pretty innocent behaviour that gets caught. Like me, you may have suffered the shame of being told off for over-enthusiastic visits to your favourite shopping website during your lunch break (OK, or at any other time during the day) or for placing just one too many desperate calls to the *Who Wants to be a Millionaire* competition line over the office phone.

But can our bosses rap our knuckles for doing this – and what rights do we have to stop them? Doesn't the law provide a balance between your employer's right to know what's going on and your own right to privacy? Sadly, that's always been a delicate question, and it looks like the conflict may go head to head over the next few months.

Like many of us, you may have thought the Human Rights Act would improve your freedom in the workplace – but then, if you've read about the controversial Regulation of Investigatory Powers Act (or 'RIP': scary name, scary piece of law), you may decide Big Brother has won the fight before it even began. These two conflicting bits of legislation may affect your life at work.

Email/Internet monitoring

A whole host of computer programs allow employers to search for keywords in emails, read your correspondence and register the Internet sites you visit. Again, your boss will come up with a range of reasons why monitoring is necessary, like security, protection of the company's image etc etc. But in practice, it still feels like you're being spied on.

Before the RIP code, employers were generally pretty careful to monitor emails only where they believed both the sender and the recipient were aware of the possibility that their correspondence wasn't private. But now your company can check your email without consent for various purposes, like recording evidence of business transactions; monitoring standards of training and service or preventing unauthorised use of the computer system.

> *A whole host of computer programs allow employers to search for keywords in emails, read your correspondence and register the Internet sites you visit*

All sounds quite innocent – but in practice, it covers a multitude of sins. You can sympathise with firms who have ended up paying out millions for racist or sexist emails they have no idea their staff are circulating. (In America, oil firm Chevron stumped up $2.2 million when lawyers looking for dirt in a sexual harassment claim dug up a couple of slightly risque emails.) But again, surely it's possible to put some system in place to monitor dodgy messages like that without trawling through all your personal email?

Though the answer may be yes in theory, in practice employers may want to review all messages at will. In America, over half of all corporate email systems are monitored, and that trend is already on the increase in the UK.

CCTV

The use of CCTV in the workplace isn't currently regulated under UK law, although the government has published a voluntary code of practice. This contains various helpful bits of advice. It asks employers to:
- position cameras so that they only capture relevant images
- put up signs to say that CCTV is in use UNLESS the cameras are

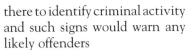
there to identify criminal activity and such signs would warn any likely offenders

■ ensure that they don't record conversations between employees

■ retain data for 28 days and then wipe clean and reuse the tape

■ allow employees to see the recorded images.

So far, so good. But unfortunately the code is voluntary and there's nothing much you can do to make your employer follow it. All in all, not very encouraging. If you're caught on camera, realistically your only other option is to argue that in filming you, your employer has damaged your faith in the employment relationship – and you could resign and sue. If you win your case, you could come out of this pretty well in financial terms. But it's still a pretty dramatic response to have to make.

Phone-tapping

Lots of employers routinely tap telephones. They argue it helps to assess employee performance, ensure customer satisfaction and record evidence of business transactions. Again, a blatant breach of what most believe is a right to privacy at work. Your boss could be listening in to details of what your boyfriend's going to be cooking for your supper, or discovering just how irate your bank manager is about your overdraft. Surely, this time, there's something you can do about it? Sorry – the RIP code allows your employer to tap your phone, on the same grounds that emails can be monitored.

Human Rights Act

So, is the Human Rights Act going to help in the fight against RIP and Big Brother? On the face of it, the Act gives you a number of rights – including respect for your private and family life, your home and your correspondence. Sounds good – the monitoring of phone calls, emails and the use of CCTV all potentially breach these freedoms. But the Act only applies directly to public employers – and even here, there are a number of defences. If your employer:

■ sets out the manner in which it expects its email, Internet and telephones to be used;

■ informs staff that they may be monitored in certain circumstances; and

■ the monitoring is done on a reasonable level the chances are none of the above will be breaching your human rights.

So, Big Brother is most definitely out there. Do you play him at his own game, or do you stick your neck out and risk getting the boot? The safe advice must be to use your company phone and computer reasonably – employers will rarely dismiss on the basis of only moderate personal use of their equipment. Your employer should be making it quite clear to you what is and what isn't acceptable use of its systems – if it doesn't, chances are any action it takes against you won't be lawful.

It's definitely true to say that companies are worried about the effect of heavy-handed monitoring on staff morale. But, like me, you may still find it deeply disturbing that they're monitoring everything you do – and that they can get away with it.

■ The above information is reprinted with kind permission from iVillage UK. Visit www.ivillage.co.uk for more information.

© iVillage UK

They are watching YOU

Information from the *New Internationalist*

The Pentagon calls it total information awareness and it's coming to your neighbourhood soon. Information is being gathered about you and stored in an easily searchable database. There are now over five million people on the US MASTER TERROR WATCHLIST. You say you haven't done anything wrong. But can you prove it?

Closed circuit TV

Britain leads the way here with an estimated million cameras already in place. But other industrial countries are quick to follow. It's hard to go anywhere (at least anywhere urban) without being caught on video. It used to be just banks, police stations and sensitive government buildings. But now you get to 'star' in your own life in all kinds of places. Airports, train stations, shopping malls: you are on candid camera! Since 9/11 there have been attempts to link up CCTV with other identification technologies. The Visionics FaceIt technology being deployed in Boston's Logan Airport, for example, compares facial characteristics of travellers, airport employees and flight crews with those of known terrorists. The 100,000-plus crowd at the 2001 Superbowl in Tampa, Florida, was scanned and 19 petty criminals were recognised. But the idea of adapting CCTV to biometrics to discover identities has real limits – it is projected that to find one terrorist there would need to be 9,999 false alarms.

Biometrics

This is a relatively recent 'identification' technology which figures out who you are by using unique physical attributes such as fingerprints, irises, retinas, hand geometry, vein patterns or voices. Some testing of biometric indicators is taking place at airports from Amsterdam to Sydney. Biometrics are at the heart of schemes by various governments to introduce a national ID 'smart' card to make sure you are who you say you are – as well as a legitimate reason for being where you are.

They are also being advanced as a way of protecting passports against forgery. Biometrics are sometimes combined with something called Radio Frequency Identification (RFID) – little tags that can give off a signal to identify either products or people at a distance. These are already used to keep track of prisoners and are currently under consideration for passports and driving licences.

Any totalitarian state worth its salt insists that you carry 'papers' at all times

---

National identity cards

Any totalitarian state worth its salt insists that you carry 'papers' at all times. The Twin Towers attack has added new fuel to the push for national identity cards in democratic countries. Smart card schemes are already in development in Britain, Germany, Spain and Malaysia. Partisans of the identity card envisage it merging commercial and security functions so that without it you cannot get a job, board a plane, check into a hotel, cash a cheque or even log on to the internet. But cards are more effective in identifying whole classes of people through 'social sorting' (immigrants, a particular ethnic group, those receiving state benefit) than in exposing individual terrorists. In Nazi-occupied Europe subjugated peoples were forced to carry papers proving their racial status.

Your PC is no longer personal

It used to be that private communication could be breached only by steaming open your letters or wiretapping your phone. These measures were (at least in theory) restricted by judicial oversight. But since 9/11 the authorities have a lot more scope to intercept private communication. The email you send and the websites you visit can be monitored via your service provider. This is a point where commercial and government tracking meet. The former wants to keep track of your consumer preferences for marketing

purposes while the latter desires to know your movements, contacts and ideas. A series of interlocking technologies vacuums up a huge amount of personal and commercial information from all over the globe. Among them is a system of linked satellite tracking stations called Echelon that sifts through the world's phone conversations for key words. Such technologies are in danger of data overload and in any case are more effective in proving guilt than in stopping terrorist or criminal acts before they occur.

Eye in the sky

Another form of highly secretive surveillance involves remote-sensing satellites. Geospatial intelligence is the science of combining imagery, such as satellite pictures, to depict physically features or activities happening anywhere on the planet. Such satellite systems evolved during the Cold War primarily to provide military intelligence. But particularly since 9/11 they have been used for much broader purposes. In 2003 they were used to target and kill suspected members of al-Qaeda in a remote part of Yemen. Most such surveillance takes place over 'hostile' territory. But a little-known branch of the US Defense Department – the National Geospatial Intelligence Agency – is involved in surveillance of US domestic events such as political conventions as well as sensitive potential targets like nuclear power stations. The technology is spreading fast. China is planning to have 100 such satellites in the air by 2020 to keep track of 'various activities of

society'. But if these systems are so effective, why haven't they found Osama bin Laden?

Are you on the 'no fly' list?

Airports have become the meeting point of the new techniques in surveillance. They combine the commercial observation carried out by airlines (from credit cards to passenger histories) with the state surveillance connected to border controls and airport security. Several schemes for an overall international passenger database are being developed that would maintain searchable data on millions of people. In the US a couple of versions of CAPPS (The Computer Assisted Passenger Pre-Screening Index) have proved too controversial but a new one benignly entitled Secure Flight is in the works. A 'passenger threat index' evaluates the threat each passenger poses. Already 'no fly lists' have led to the holding and questioning of US antiwar activists on domestic flights. Increasingly airports are connected to global networks of security information-sharing. This globalisation of surveillance information can lead to some very nasty surprises, as Canadians of Syrian and Egyptian origin found out when they were held and tortured in their respective countries of birth due to information provided by Western security services.
March 2005

Q&A: Identity cards

Simon Jeffery explains the issues surrounding the UK's proposed ID cards scheme

Are we going to get identity cards?

The government certainly wants us to. It has been suggesting the need for identity cards, or some euphemistically-titled variant such as 'entitlement cards', for some years and legislation to set up a scheme is now before parliament. Today's key vote is on whether the cards should be compulsory for all passport holders, following an amendment passed last month in the Lords to make participation entirely voluntary.

Why?

The scheme's supporters claim the cards will counter identity fraud, and so help to control illegal immigration and working, identity theft, the misuse of public services and issues around organised crime and terrorism.

The Lords amendment is crucial to the scheme eventually running as the government wants it to. Registering passport applicants was intended to bring participation to 80% by 2013, when a further decision would then be made on whether to make the cards compulsory (which by then would be compulsory in all but name only, especially if non-passport holders were using standalone identity cards to access public services). If there is an opt-out for passport holders, the calculation changes.

How is the scheme intended to work?

It comes in two parts. The cards, and – more importantly – the national identity register that will back them up. The database will be the biggest of its kind in the UK, the biggest public sector IT project in Europe, and will hold information on every British resident, including everywhere they have ever lived and every number, such as NHS or national insurance number, that the government has ever issued to them. The use of biometric data, such as digitally-encoded fingerprints, is supposed

to make the system less susceptible to forgery than its non-biometric equivalents. Supporters claim the British scheme will become a gold standard for identity cards.

In hospitals, police stations and social security offices across Britain, electronic readers will then connect scanned cards to the database in order to prove the bearer's identity. A series of fines and custodial sentences will then be introduced to keep cardholders in check and keep the information on the register up to date – £1,000 for failing to disclose a change of address, or up to 10 years' jail for fraudulent use of the card.

Will it work?

In the light of the Home Office's sometimes troubled relationship with large IT projects, there must be some doubt over the proposals. In general, databases become less secure the larger they get (because more people have access to them), so the national identity register would be more vulnerable than most. As a gold standard for identity cards, it will inevitably attract hackers and organised criminals hoping to pierce the outer armour. Whether they succeed or not will depend on how their ingenuity fares against that of those charged with defending it.

Is it necessary?

The government case rests on two propositions. First, that identity fraud is growing (the Home Office estimates the cost at £1.7bn annually) and therefore something needs to be done to tackle it. Second, that with European countries and the US moving to biometric passports, much of the work necessary to build and run the scheme will be happening already.

That overstates the case somewhat since the British proposals are the most ambitious of their kind (biometric US passports are not even using fingerprints, just a digital photograph).

Some critics of the scheme acknowledge that identity cards could have benefits for cardholders, but are concerned about the reliance on a centralised database. The author of the safety and security sections of a critical London School of Economics report on the scheme, a former Nato defence specialist called Brian Gladman, said he backed an 'irrevocably voluntary, self-funded ID card scheme' but worried the government proposals would compromise the security of anyone whose details were entered on the database.

Claims that identity cards would help in the fight against terrorism were seemingly punctured when Charles Clarke, the home secretary, said they would not have stopped the July 7 London suicide attacks. However, this was already the government's position. Tony Blair conceded in November 2004 the cards could be an important weapon in cases in which false identities were used, rather than a 'silver bullet' to defeat terrorism.

How much will it cost?

No one knows. Or at least no one is saying. The same LSE report contributed to by Brian Gladman put the cost at £12bn to £18bn over 10 years, and was duly savaged by the government. The initial government estimates were for £3.1bn, but that could be the cost of Home Office spending alone. Ministers say 70% of the cost will be spent on biometric passports whether the cards are introduced or not. Some of the cost will be carried by individuals, with a combined passport/ID application costing a possible £93. By comparison, an ID card in Germany costs 8 euros (£5.50). A UK passport currently costs £51. The Lords have insisted on a government report outlining the full cost estimate of the card and registration scheme before the bill can come into force. The costs would then be subject to the approval of the auditor general and the Commons.

Do the Commons support identity cards?

The Tories and the Liberal Democrats are opposed to the scheme. As the governing party, Labour would be expected to support it, but Tony Blair and the home secretary, Charles Clarke, have not always been able to rely on Labour backbenchers to back them over identity cards. The bill was scuppered by a lack of time when the government tried to push it through the last parliament (19 of its backbenchers also voted against it). Labour's majority was a lot larger before the 2005 general election than the 64 seats it has now, so getting the legislation through this parliament will be harder.

What are the arguments against?

Most opponents object to identity cards on the basis that they are a solution in search of a problem – that they are an end in themselves and, as such, the collection of large amounts of personal data is an unwarranted intrusion. The money, they argue, could instead be spent on police or the security services to better protect the country against terrorism and crime.

The database itself raises concerns. First, that function-creep would see more personal details from different government departments – such as health and tax records – merged onto a central file. Second, that a more informal kind of function-creep will be unavoidable as banks and other agencies create a network of so-called satellite databases to cross-reference credit ratings and home ownership status against the national identity register. The draft legislation encourages such checking and suggests 'identity verification services' could cover part of the running costs.

Richard Thomas, the information commissioner, who is charged with making sure the information stored on British databases is strictly proportionate to their use, has expressed concerns that the proposals go much further than is necessary to implement a straightforward identity scheme. He says the government has changed its line over the cards so many times that there is no longer 'clarity' over its intentions.

Lord Phillips, a Liberal Democrat who led opposition to the bill in the Lords, said the bill was 'going to undermine the relationship between the state and the citizen, which is already weakened and mistrustful'.

Have we ever had identity cards here before?

Wartime identity cards were abandoned in 1952 after Clarence Willcock, a motorist from north London, took PC Harold Muckle to court for demanding his papers. Mr Willcock had been asked to pull over to the kerb and hand over some ID, but he refused and was charged. A judge later ruled that police should not demand identity papers as a matter of routine.

Since then, there have been a number of attempts to reintroduce identity cards to remedy the political concerns of the day. In 1989, the Home Office commissioned a feasibility study into a national system of voluntary identity cards intended to combat crime and the IRA. In 1991, Kenneth Baker, the then home secretary, urged banks and building societies to consider adopting a common photocard for customers to prove their identity.

Michael Howard, one of Mr Baker's successors, told the 1994 Tory party conference that he supported a voluntary scheme (and was heckled by pro-compulsory delegates). In the last twitch of the Tories' ID card tail, John Major announced in 1995 that a compulsory card scheme was at the top of the list of priorities in his fight against crime. All these schemes were quietly dropped.

Labour's interest in the idea of ID cards began in September 2001, in the wake of the terrorist attacks on the US, when the then home secretary, David Blunkett, proposed a system of compulsory cards. However, the legislation to introduce them was left out of emergency anti-terrorism bills. Asylum seekers were then issued with identity cards in 2002, the same year in which Mr Blunkett said that an 'entitlement card' could help tackle illegal working and the misuse of public services.

What happens elsewhere?

Many countries operate either a voluntary or compulsory identity card scheme. France has a voluntary card that is used to prove entitlement to some public services.

The US has no national scheme but, in practice, driving licences are used to prove identity and a new bill seeks to add immigration status to the information held by state licensing authorities.

Australia attempted to introduce an identity card in 1987, but the government backed down in the face of an organised campaign against the plan.

13 February 2006

"I BELIEVE THE ID CARD WILL PROTECT MY FREEDOM AND PRIVACY"

ID cards and human rights

ID cards 'could fall foul of human rights law'

Compulsory national identity cards raise 'serious questions' about the protection of individual privacy under human rights law, MPs and peers said yesterday.

The Government's plans could also breach legislation forbidding discrimination by making some people subject to the ID regime while others are, for the time being, exempt. In a report, the joint parliamentary committee on human rights casts fresh doubt on Government claims that an ID card would help tackle crime, terrorism and illegal immigration.

Under Article 8 of the European Convention on Human Rights, interference in private lives must be justified by a 'pressing social need'

It points out that the phased introduction of the cards and the accompanying National Identity Register will mean that a compulsory scheme, with penalties for non-compliance, will exist alongside a voluntary one.

By Philip Johnston, Home Affairs Editor

From 2007, anyone renewing a passport will automatically be issued with an ID card and number, while those who do not need a new passport or do not possess one will not be subject to the regime.

The European Convention on Human Rights – which Labour incorporated into law in 1998 – does not bar ID cards but the committee suggests that ministers' plans to gather and record personal data go further than the law allows.

Under Article 8 of the convention, interference in private lives must be justified by a 'pressing social need' and it has to be shown that the aims cannot be achieved by less intrusive means.

The committee says the details that can be held on the register, including previous addresses, travel abroad and records of the occasions on which such information has been provided to other agencies, would potentially provide 'a detailed picture of private life'.

The European Court of Human Rights has already ruled that holding information concerning an individual's distant past raises issues under Article 8. The Government maintains that the details to be held are unexceptionable and available elsewhere.

The ID Card Bill, now before Parliament, would allow for an 'audit trail' of the occasions on which the register has been accessed, something the committee considered to be 'potentially highly intrusive of privacy'. The report also points to powers in the legislation that would allow biometric data already held on individuals, such as fingerprints, to be transferred without permission to the register.

The report goes on to challenge the basis of the scheme's introduction through passports. As the ID card is phased in there will be those required by law to have a card and to be registered, and those for whom it is not a requirement. The committee said this could be a breach of Article 14 of the convention which prohibits 'unjustified discrimination on any grounds'.

Overall, the committee is unconvinced that the Government has shown, as it must under human rights laws, that an ID card and a register would achieve aims and benefits that outweigh the intrusion into civil liberties.

Simon Hughes, of the Liberal Democrats, said: 'This committee expresses deep dissatisfaction that the Government has not explained how its ID card plans are compatible with human rights.'

3 February 2005

Deportation will not save Europe from terrorism

By Ben Ward, Special Counsel to the Europe and Central Asia division of Human Rights Watch

Western European governments grappling with terrorism seem to have settled on a swift and convenient method to deal with the radical clerics seen to be inciting Muslim youths into acts of terror: they simply deport them.

Across the European Union, governments are moving to expel troublesome clerics said to preach hate, together with foreign terrorism suspects. The French Interior Minister, Nicolas Sarkozy, who advocates the expulsion of foreign residents convicted of participating in the recent rioting, has long endorsed deporting Islamist radicals deemed a threat to national security. Sarkozy championed a change in French law last year that allows the authorities to expel foreigners who incite 'discrimination, hate or violence against a specific person or group of persons', a measure designed to target radical Muslim clerics. France has expelled at least six imams since the law entered into force in July 2004.

France is not alone in its enthusiasm for expulsion. German states such as Bavaria are making use of a January 1, 2005, federal law that allows them to expel legal foreign residents who 'endorse or promote terrorist acts', or incite hatred against sections of the population. In August, the British government broadened the grounds for deportation to enable it to remove persons who 'justify or glorify' terrorism. Italy has expelled at least five imams since 2003, and an anti-terrorism law adopted on July 31, 2005, makes it even easier to do so.

Britain is determined to deport undesirables even when it means breaching international law. It has moved to deport terrorism suspects to countries where they face torture, based on 'diplomatic assurances' from the receiving government, despite clear evidence that these promises are an ineffective safeguard against such treatment. London has already signed 'no-torture' agreements with Jordan and Libya, and negotiations are under way with other governments with poor records on torture.

The danger of these measures is illustrated by the case of two Egyptians returned by Sweden in 2001 after 'no-torture' promises from Cairo. There is credible evidence that both men were tortured in detention, despite visits from Swedish diplomats. In May, the UN torture committee found that Sweden had violated international law in the case.

The deadly attacks in Madrid and London underscore that Europe faces a real threat from terrorism. And expressions of hatred and violence, especially by those in positions of influence, are reprehensible. But deportation is not the answer. Terrorism is criminal activity – far better to prosecute those involved than to export the problem. Where there is insufficient evidence, those who are deemed a threat can be put under surveillance, with appropriate judicial safeguards.

Why don't governments go this route? Building a case is painstaking work. And criminal defendants have rights. By relying on deportation – an immigration measure – governments can bypass the safeguards built into the criminal justice system. In France and Germany, for example, lodging an appeal with the administrative court does not automatically suspend the expulsion, while the new rules in Italy mean people have the right to appeal only after they have been deported. The absence of an appeal before removal increases the risk that a person will be sent back to face torture. While some high-profile expulsion cases have been overturned on appeal, there is little doubt that deportation is far easier to achieve than conviction in a criminal court.

The ease with which the policy of deportation can be pursued, however, should not blind us to its costs. Deportation is a deeply counterproductive answer to terrorism. Muslim leaders across Europe

have signalled concern that expelling Muslim clerics for non-violent speech reinforces the view that Islam is synonymous with terrorism, and sends a signal to Muslim communities that they are not welcome in Europe, risking further alienation among the region's young Muslim citizens. That is doubly true where a person is sent back to face torture, a practice that undermines more than half a century of efforts to rid the world of that moral cancer.

EU leaders will meet in Brussels on December 15 and 16 to discuss the EU action plan on counter-terrorism, including ways to prevent the radicalisation of young people and how to stop them from being drawn toward terrorism. They are right to do so. But deportation is likely to have the opposite effect. Far better to rely on the measures that helped make Europe a beacon for freedom around the world – a fair criminal justice system, tolerance for an open debate, and respect for fundamental rights, including protection from torture.

■ The above information is reprinted with kind permission from Human Rights Watch. For more information, please visit the Human Rights Watch website at www.hrw.org.

© Human Rights Watch

Highest court rules out use of torture evidence

Decision affirms global ban on torture

The unanimous ruling by Britain's highest court that torture evidence can never be used in court proceedings is an important milestone, Human Rights Watch said today.

'This is a real victory in the struggle against torture,' said Holly Cartner, Europe and Central Asia director of Human Rights Watch. 'The Law Lords have affirmed a core tenet of our values – that torture evidence is never acceptable.'

A seven-judge panel of the House of Lords Judicial Committee (commonly known as 'the Law Lords') ruled that even in terrorism cases, no British court can consider evidence obtained under torture. In the words of Lord Nicholls: 'Torture is not acceptable. This is a bedrock moral principle in this country.' The verdict overturns an August 2004 majority decision by the Court of Appeal that such evidence could be used, provided that the UK 'neither procured nor connived at' the torture.

Human Rights Watch is part of a coalition of fourteen human rights and anti-torture organisations that intervened in the House of Lords case.

The British government's assertion that such evidence should be admissible is part of a growing effort to erode the torture prohibition.

It is seeking to bypass the ban on returning people to torture by obtaining promises of humane treatment to allow it to deport terrorism suspects, despite clear evidence that such promises are an ineffective safeguard. It has concluded no-torture agreements with Jordan and Libya, and is negotiating similar ones with Egypt, Algeria and other countries with poor records on torture.

'Britain's highest court has sent a clear signal to the government that torture is wrong,' said Cartner. 'It is vital that the British government heeds that message at last, and stops trying to undermine the global torture ban.'

The case, *A and others*, was brought by ten foreign nationals previously certified under the Anti-Terrorism Crime and Security Act 2001 as suspected international terrorists and subject to indefinite detention without trial. The majority of the men are Algerian. In December 2004, the Law Lords ruled that indefinite detention was unlawful. The case arises from a July 2002 decision by the Special Immigration Appeals Commission (SIAC) that it was entitled to consider evidence that may have been obtained under torture in determining the men's appeals against certification. The certifications will now be reconsidered by the SIAC in light of the House of Lords judgment.

Two of the men have left the UK and two had their certificates revoked prior to December 2004. Six of the men were subject to control orders under the Prevention of Terrorism Act 2005 following their release from indefinite detention in March 2005, but an unspecified number of the six were subsequently detained on immigration charges pending their deportation on national security grounds.

Members of the coalition that intervened in the case are: the AIRE Centre, Amnesty International, the Association for the Prevention of Torture, British Irish Rights Watch, The Committee on the Administration of Justice, Doctors for Human Rights, Human Rights Watch, The International Federation of Human Rights, INTERIGHTS, the Law Society of England and Wales, Liberty, the Medical Foundation for the Care of Victims of Torture, REDRESS, and the World Organisation Against Torture.

8 December 2005

■ The above information is reprinted with kind permission from Human Rights Watch. Visit www.hrw.org for more information.

© Human Rights Watch

KEY FACTS

- Article 12 of the CRC states that 'any child who is capable of forming his or her views [has] the right to express those views freely in all matters affecting them'. (page 1)

- In West and Central Africa, only 55% of girls receive a primary education. (page 1)

- The standards in the Convention on the Rights of the Child were negotiated by governments, non-governmental organisations, human rights advocates, lawyers, health specialists, social workers, educators, child development experts and religious leaders from all over the world, over a 10-year period. (page 4)

- The Convention on the Rights of the Child is the most widely and rapidly ratified human rights treaty in history. Only two countries, Somalia and the United States, have not ratified this celebrated agreement. (page 5)

- Article 12 of the Convention on the Rights of the Child states that children have the right to participate in decision-making processes that may be relevant in their lives and to influence decisions taken in their regard – within the family, the school or the community. (page 9)

- Children are full-fledged persons who have the right to express their views in all matters affecting them. (page 9)

- 23% of 11- to 21-year-olds questioned said they would be 'absolutely certain to vote' in the next general election. (page 10)

- Over 50% of children in custody have been in care, 70% have suffered abuse and 90% have mental-health problems. (page 12)

- Britain imprisons more young people than almost any other country in Europe – despite the fact that there is no corresponding increase in serious youth crime. (page 12)

- It is estimated that between 100 and 150 million children live on the street, the majority of whom are adolescents. (page 13)

- Girls experiencing early pregnancy and childbirth risk severe complications or even death as a result of the stress on their immature bodies. Globally, girls aged 15-19 are twice as likely to die in childbirth as women in their twenties. And girls aged 10-14 are five times as likely to die. (page 13)

- It is estimated that 246 million under-18s are engaged in child labour, and two-thirds of them – 171 million – are doing work that is hazardous. (page 14)

- The majority of working children are in agriculture – an estimated 70 per cent. Child domestic work in the houses of others is thought to be the single largest employer of girls worldwide. (page 18)

- Most children work because their families are poor and their labour is necessary for their survival. Discrimination on grounds including gender, race or religion also plays its part in why some children work. (page 17)

- 73 million working children are less than 10 years old. (page 19)

- Sub-Saharan Africa has the largest proportion of working children: nearly one-third of children age 14 and under (48 million children). (page 19)

- At least 12.3 million people are trapped in forced labour around the world. (page 28)

- Millions of men, women and children around the world are forced to lead lives as slaves. Although this exploitation is often not called slavery, the conditions are the same. People are sold like objects, forced to work for little or no pay and are at the mercy of their 'employers'. (page 29)

- Enshrined in Article 14 of the 1948 Universal Declaration of Human Rights is the right 'to seek and to enjoy in other countries asylum from persecution'. (page 31)

- A whole host of computer programs allow employers to search for keywords in emails, read your correspondence and register the Internet sites you visit. (page 32)

- Britain leads the way in CCTV camera installation with an estimated million cameras already in place. (page 33)

- Supporters of the ID card scheme claim the cards will counter identity fraud, and so help to control illegal immigration and working, identity theft, the misuse of public services and issues around organised crime and terrorism. (page 35)

- Most opponents object to identity cards on the basis that they are a solution in search of a problem – that they are an end in themselves and, as such, the collection of large amounts of personal data is an unwarranted intrusion. The money, they argue, could instead be spent on police or the security services. (page 36)

GLOSSARY

Big Brother
A figure in George Orwell's *1984*, representing the constant surveillance of individuals. The term is often used in relation to breaches of our right to privacy. This is also the name of a popular reality television show in which contestants are constantly monitored by hidden cameras.

Biometrics
An identification technology which works out who you are by using unique physical attributes such as fingerprints and irises.

Bonded labour
A form of modern slavery. People become bonded labourers by taking or being tricked into taking a loan. To repay the debt, many are forced to work long hours with only basic food and shelter for 'payment'. They may never pay off the loan.

Child labour
Some children across the world are exploited for economic reasons. They can be made to perform work whihc is dangerous, interferes with their education or is harmful to the child's health or physical, mental, spiritual, moral or social development.

Children's rights
A set of entitlements for all children, of whatever age and background. Most children's rights advocates use the UN Convention on the Rights of the Child (CRC) as their guide to children's human rights.

Child soldiers
There are about 300,000 child soldiers involved in over 30 areas of conflict worldwide, some even younger than 10 years old. Child soldiers fight on the front line, and also work in support roles; girls are often obliged to be sex slaves or 'soldiers' wives'.

Forced labour
A form of modern slavery affecting people who are illegally recruited by individuals, governments or political parties and forced to work – usually under threat of violence or other penalties.

Forced marriage
A form of modern slavery affecting women and girls who are married without choice and forced into lives of servitude. This is often accompanied by physical violence.

Human rights
Basic human rights are founded on the concept that all people should enjoy freedom of speech, freedom from tyranny and oppression, and should have fair legal treatment. They should not be discriminated against on grounds of race, colour, sex, language, religion, nationality, political opinion, or other status. (Definition from www.thesite.org.)

The Human Rights Act 1998
A binding international agreement which enshrines fundamental civil and political rights. From October 2000, this Act made rights from the European Convention on Human Rights enforceable in UK courts.

Millennium Declaration
A commitment to development, peace and human rights.

Physical punishment, or 'smacking'
Physical punishment is the use of physical force with the intention of causing a child to experience pain, but not injury, to correct or control the child's behaviour.

Refugees
Someone with a well-founded fear of persecution on the basis of his or her race, religion, nationality, membership in a particular social group or political opinion, who is outside of his or her country of nationality and unable or unwilling to return.

The Regulation of Investigatory Powers Act 2000 (RIP)
A law covering interception of communications such as email and phone calls. Some feel it encroaches on our civil liberties.

Slavery by descent
When people are born into a slave class or from a 'group' that society views as suited to being used as slave labour.

Trafficking
Trafficking involves transporting people away from the communities in which they live, by the threat or use of violence, deception or coercion so they can be exploited as forced or enslaved workers for sex or labour.

UN Convention on the Rights of the Child
The Convention spells out children's rights and asks countries to protect these rights. Children are definied as persons up to the age of 18 years. 192 countries have ratified this convention.

The Universal Declaration of Human Rights
A declaration adopted by the United Nations General Assembly in 1948, outlining the basic human rights which should be afforded to all.

INDEX

ADDITIONAL RESOURCES

Other Issues *titles*

If you are interested in researching further the issues raised in *The Human Rights Issue*, you may want to read the following titles in the **Issues** series as they contain additional relevant articles:

- Vol. 22 *Confronting Child Abuse* (ISBN 1 86168 178 X)
- Vol. 71 *Abortion* (ISBN 1 86168 253 0)
- Vol. 82 *Protecting our Privacy* (ISBN 1 86168 277 8)
- Vol. 89 *Refugees* (ISBN 1 86168 290 5)
- Vol. 99 *Exploited Children* (ISBN 1 86168 313 8)
- Vol. 102 *The Ethics of Euthanasia* (ISBN 1 86168 316 2)
- Vol. 103 *Animal Rights* (ISBN 1 86168 317 0)
- Vol. 110 *Poverty* (ISBN 1 86168 343 X)
- Vol. 121 *The Censorship Debate* (ISBN 1 86168 354 5)

For more information about these titles, visit our website at www.independence.co.uk/publicationslist

Useful organisations

You may find the websites of the following organisations useful for further research:

- Anti-slavery International: www.antislavery.org
- The British Institute of Human Rights: www.bihr.org
- Children 1st: www.children1st.org.uk
- The Children's Rights Alliance for England: www.crae.org.uk
- Human Rights Watch: www.hrw.org
- The International Labour Organization: www.ilo.org
- Plan UK: www.plan-uk.org.uk
- UNICEF: www.unicef.org.uk

ACKNOWLEDGEMENTS

The publisher is grateful for permission to reproduce the following material.

While every care has been taken to trace and acknowledge copyright, the publisher tenders its apology for any accidental infringement or where copyright has proved untraceable. The publisher would be pleased to come to a suitable arrangement in any such case with the rightful owner.

Chapter One: Young People's Rights

Frequently asked questions about children's rights, © Children's Rights Alliance for England, *Children's rights timeline*, © UNICEF, *Convention on the Rights of the Child*, © UNICEF, *Excluded from democratic debate*, © British Institute of Human Rights, *The right to participation*, © UNICEF, *Children's groups warn punishment not a panacea*, © Guardian Newspapers Ltd 2006, *Youth justice – the facts*, © Barnardo's, *I'm a teenager, what happened to my rights?*, © Plan UK, *Human rights at school*, © Telegraph group Ltd 2006, *State-sanctioned violence?*, © Guardian Newspapers Ltd 2005, *Child labour*, © Anti-Slavery International, *Key statistics on child labour*, © International Labour Organization, *Children and physical punishment*, © Children 1st.

Chapter Two: Human and Civil Rights

The Universal Declaration of Human Rights, © OHCHR, *Human Rights Act*, © Crown copyright is reproduced with the permission of Her Majesty's Stationery Office, *ILO releases major new study on forced labour*, © International Labour Organization, *What is modern slavery*, © Anti-Slavery International 2006, *Modern forms of slavery in industrialized countries*, © International Labour Organization, *Refugees*, © Human Rights Watch, *Big Brother at work*, © iVillage UK, *They are watching YOU*, © New Internationalist, *Q&A: Identity cards*, © Guardian Newspapers Ltd 2006, *ID cards and human rights*, © Telegraph Group Ltd 2006, *Deportation will not save Europe from terrorism*, © Human Rights Watch, *Highest court rules out use of torture evidence*, © Human Rights Watch.

Photographs and illustrations:

Pages 1, 16: Bev Aisbett; pages 6, 11, 26, 36: Angelo Madrid; pages 8, 14, 32, 37: Simon Kneebone; pages 9, 27, 34, 38: Don Hatcher; page 23: Pumpkin House.

Craig Donnellan
Cambridge
April, 2006